WHALE
WATCHING

WHALE WATCHING

IN AUSTRALIAN & NEW ZEALAND WATERS

PETER GILL & CECILIA BURKE
Colour Illustrations by Pieter Folkens

NEW
HOLLAND

Dedicated to Bill Dawbin, 1921–1998, whose restless
energy revealed so much about whales and dolphins,
and to Maureen Burke.

First published in Australia in 1999 by
New Holland Publishers (Australia) Pty Ltd
Sydney • Auckland • London • Cape Town

14 Aquatic Drive, Frenchs Forest NSW 2086, Australia
218 Lake Road, Northcote Auckland, New Zealand
24 Nutford Place, London W1H 6DQ, United Kingdom
80 McKenzie Street, Cape Town 8001, South Africa

National Library of Australia Cataloguing-in-Publication Data
Gill, Peter
Whale watching in Australian & New Zealand waters.

Bibliography.
Includes index.

ISBN 1 86436 472 6.

1. Dolphins – Australia – Identification. 2. Dolphins – New Zealand – Identification.
3. Whales – Australia – Identification. 4. Whales – New Zealand – Identification.
5. Porpoises – Australia – Identification. 6. Porpoises – New Zealand – Identification.
I Folkens, Pieter. II. Burke, Cecilia. III. Title.
599.5

Publishing General Manager: Jane Hazell
Publisher: Averill Chase
Project Manager: Fiona Doig
Editors: Fiona Doig, Joanna Munnelly, Siobhan O'Connor, Lynn Cole
Designers: Tricia McCallum, Angela Hempstead
Maps: Colin Wynter Seton, Tricia McCallum
Picture Researcher: Raquel Hill
Reproduction by: DNL Resources
Printed by: Kyodo Printing, Singapore

page ii: *Southern right whales off Head of Bight, SA*
page vi: *Long-finned pilot whales*
page viii: *Humpback whale*
page ix: *Killer whales, mother and calf*

pages x–xii: *Humpback whales in*
            Hervey Bay, Queensland.
pages 30–31:   *Orcas*
pages 64–65:   *Bottlenose dolphins*

CONTENTS

CONTENTS

HOW TO USE THIS BOOK

 Whales and dolphins hold a special place in the hearts and minds of people. The sea is the most mysterious of Earth's domains, and no less mysterious are these graceful marine mammals, which wander it freely, seeming to embody qualities of power, vivacity and self sufficiency. The urge to discover these creatures in the wild has risen and since the late 1980s, there has been a dramatic increase in whale watching in Australia and New Zealand, both as an organised industry and by individuals. The buoyant interest in whales reflects the recovery of certain species from whaling and changing public attitudes. At certain times of year and in certain places, you can be almost guaranteed to see whales and dolphins (collectively called cetaceans), either during migration or in areas where they feed or breed. On sighting them, people often have little idea of what species they are looking at, why they are in certain areas, or what they are doing.

This book is intended as a practical guide for anyone intending to go whale watching. The first section introduces cetaceans and gives an outline of their biology, ecology and behaviour, and explains how they adapted to life in water. It reveals the grim history of whaling in Australian and NZ waters, and explores conservation issues. It also covers the development of whale research and the questions it raises.

The second section is designed to make quick and easy identifications of most cetacean species found in this region. Illustrations, maps and descriptions aid the often difficult task of identifying whales and dolphins sighted at sea or found stranded.

The next section contains a directory of the best known whale-watching sites in Australia and NZ, detailing how to get there and what species to look out for. While not an exhaustive list, as almost any headland can provide a good vantage point at the right time, this is the first book with a comprehensive guide to the best sites in Australia and NZ. The relative merits of whale watching from land or boat are discussed, together with practical matters such as recording sightings and what to do if you encounter stranded whales.

Finally, the Resources section lists relevant tourism contacts, cetacean organisations and web sites; the Glossary defines terms used in the book, many of which are specific to cetaceans; and the Further Reading list is there to further your knowledge of these fascinating animals.

UNDERSTANDING WHALES

WHAT ARE WHALES?

A pod of fin whales nosing between icebergs in a roaring Antarctic gale, an Irrawaddy dolphin exploring among mangrove roots in a Northern Territory creek, or a Gray's beaked whale hunting squid in a deep submarine canyon – all these creatures are whales. In our modern age of information, most of us are exposed to images of whales at one time or another. Yet relatively few know where whales fit into animal classification, or of the astonishing variety of species. So what are whales?

Whales are mammals and they are grouped in their own Order, the Cetacea, together with dolphins and porpoises, although, rather confusingly, all of these animals may sometimes be referred to as whales. The term is derived from the Greek "ketos", and the Latin "cetus", both meaning large sea creature or monster. Cetaceans appear to have evolved from a group of primitive land mammals called mesonychids that also gave rise to hoofed grazing mammals. According to the fossil record, cetacean ancestors returned to the water and evolved into recognisable forms over 50 million years ago. Along with the dugong and manatees, these are the marine mammals most completely adapted to an aquatic existence, as seals spend much of their time on land or ice.

Opposite: Whale watchers reach out to a curious humpback in Queensland's Hervey Bay. Above: The closest terrestrial relatives of cetaceans are probably the ungulates – hoofed grazing mammals such as cows.

EVOLUTION

The 80 or so known cetacean species evolved certain adaptations to life in water, a medium that is profoundly different from air:

- Streamlining of the body for efficient movement
- The absence of hair; development of a blubber layer for insulation
- The loss of hind limbs and development of fibrous, resilient tail flukes for propulsion through the water
- Modification of the forelimbs into paddle-like flippers
- Elongation of the facial skull bones
- Migration of the nostrils to the top of the head to form one or two blowholes and changes in the skull structure
- Adaptation of the ear to hearing underwater.

The large and small of it: the great size range within the whale Order, Cetacea, is shown by this southern right whale and a group of bottlenose dolphins.

Most people are familiar with the terms "whale", "dolphin" and "porpoise". These are not hard-and-fast divisions, but are generally based on size. The larger cetaceans tend to be called whales. The smallest are dolphins and porpoises, often similar in form but can be separately grouped by several minor features. Dolphins generally fall between whales and porpoises in size, although the largest member of the oceanic dolphin family, the orca or killer whale, is termed a whale, while the smallest, Hector's dolphin, is smaller than some porpoises. So it is really an arbitrary system of common names. Is there a better way of classifying cetaceans?

About 38 million years ago, the ancestral cetaceans evolved into two groups, differentiated by their feeding methods and structures. In one group, numerous simple teeth developed, later followed by the ability to echolocate (see box on page 6). These became today's toothed whales (odontocetes), which specialise in catching relatively large prey, such as fish or squid, one at a time. All dolphins and porpoises and some of the better-known whales, such as sperm whales, pilot whales and orcas, are toothed whales. The second group adapted to feeding on vast quantities of smaller, schooling prey, such as plankton or small fish. In place of teeth, bristle-like plates evolved on their upper jaws. Called baleen, these sieve prey from mouthfuls of water. These are the present-day mysticetes – "moustached" or baleen whales – such as southern right, humpback and minke whales. Baleen whales in turn, are divided into rorquals (the groove-throated whales) and the right whales. The blowhole also distinguishes the two groups: it is single in toothed whales and double in baleen whales, producing a V-shaped blow in some species.

The range of forms and lifestyles of cetaceans is staggering. The huge blue whale – reaching 33 metres and more than 120 tonnes – is possibly the largest animal ever known to have lived. At the other extreme, Hector's dolphin reaches only 1.5 metres and weighs around 60 kilograms. Each species varies in its body, dorsal fin and fluke shape; body colouration; tooth pattern and length or number and colour of baleen plates. In addition, species differ in their behavioural and social complexities, and the ways in which they have adapted to exploit a bewildering array of aquatic environments, from the polar seas to the warm soup of equatorial rivers.

Australian and New Zealand waters are home to 44 species, which comprise members of almost all the cetacean families. That over half the world's known species live in this relatively small region indicates the generally broad distribution of cetaceans – many species occur worldwide. Australians and New Zealanders are indeed fortunate to have such cetacean diversity.

One of the several possible "family trees" showing evolutionary relationships between the cetaceans. Baleen and toothed whales evolved differences about 38 million years ago.

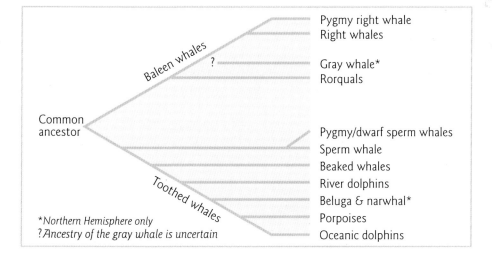

Baleen whales ?

Pygmy right whale
Right whales

Gray whale*
Rorquals

Common ancestor

Pygmy/dwarf sperm whales
Sperm whale
Beaked whales
River dolphins
Beluga & narwhal*
Porpoises
Oceanic dolphins

Toothed whales

*Northern Hemisphere only
?Ancestry of the gray whale is uncertain

BIOLOGY AND ECOLOGY

Cetaceans are among the most mobile of mammals and rarely seem to come to rest. Their movement through the water appears effortless, although of course it's not – they actually expend considerable energy, but they do it efficiently compared to most other mammals. Water has properties that both help and hinder warm-blooded aquatic animals: it's much denser than air and so supports their weight, allowing the great size of some whales, but it offers more resistance to movement and also conducts heat away from the body much more efficiently than air. The streamlined body shape of cetaceans, combined with their smooth rubbery skin, allows them to slip through the water with little turbulence. This ability is achieved by special properties of the skin that help reduce drag and enable them to use their large swimming musculature to best effect. They beat their horizontal flukes vertically in order to move and flippers are used as hydrofoils for steering, stopping and manoeuvring.

BREATHING AND DIVING

Cetaceans are voluntary breathers – unlike us, they can breathe whenever they wish, and hold their breath for extended periods. The first clue to the presence of a cetacean is often the "blow" or spout – the loud whoosh of expelled air and vapour – which in some species may be seen at a great distance, and can be heard if close enough. It is a mixture of the warm exhaled air condensing as it meets the cooler outside air, plus oil droplets from the nasal passages and whatever water may be lying around the blowholes. It has a distinctive fishy, sometimes foul, smell and inhaling it should be avoided as whales can suffer from respiratory diseases.

Cetaceans spend most of their time below the surface, usually surfacing only to breathe. Breathing patterns vary among species, according to the animals' activity and the depths to which they dive. Some dolphins spend most of their time near the surface, blowing regularly. At the other end of the spectrum, deep-diving animals, such as sperm whales, may submerge for up to two hours and then lie at the surface, blowing repeatedly as they re-oxygenate their blood and muscles. Migrating baleen whales breathe during each of several surfacings and then swim submerged for 5–15 minutes before another breathing cycle. Most cetaceans are slightly

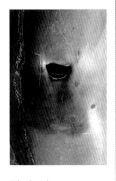

The bottlenose dolphin's single blowhole – here seen open – is closed by a nasal plug, a flap of muscular tissue, which is under the voluntary control of the dolphin.

The characteristic V-shaped blow of a southern right whale. The blow of most other baleen whale species appears as a single spout, although they have two blowholes.

negatively buoyant, which means they'll sink if they exhale and stop swimming. Others are buoyant due to abundantly thick blubber.

Cetaceans have small lungs, but to compensate for this they have muscles and blood that are rich in myoglobin, an oxygen-binding protein. They move oxygen efficiently from the lungs to the muscles while breathing at the surface. Because they do not store air in the lungs when they dive as humans do, they avoid the "bends" suffered by scuba divers, who must breathe air under pressure. In addition, whales conserve oxygen when deep diving by slowing their heartbeat and diverting blood to essential organs such as the

Overheating

Although water is a heat-sapping medium for warm-blooded animals, a major problem for cetaceans is getting rid of excess heat that is created by exercise – this is because the blubber layer is a very efficient insulator. A complex heat-exchange system of veins and arteries shunts warm blood to the skin of the flukes, dorsal fin and the flippers, allowing loss of heat into the water in a controlled manner. Consequently the skin of very active whales or dolphins may appear pink at close range, as seen here. The usually white flipper of this blue whale has become pink with the exertion of feeding. So efficient is their insulating blubber that dead stranded whales actually cook in the trapped heat of their own decomposition.

brain and heart. The feeding dives of some toothed whales are phenomenal. Sperm whales can dive to depths of 3 kilometres, where there is complete darkness and extreme pressure. As their bodies lack air spaces and are thus almost incompressible, no damage is done.

THE SENSES

Seawater is rarely very clear, so sight is of limited value, and cetaceans have evolved sophisticated hearing as their primary sense to suit this medium. However, most cetaceans have good short-range eyesight, which is valuable in identifying companions, prey, predators and other nearby objects. Some dolphins also appear to have good colour vision and some have binocular vision, while others have widely separated eyes that may see independently.

Senses of smell and taste are critical to most land mammals but of limited use to cetaceans. Baleen whales have olfactory receptors in their brains and may be able to smell plankton on the wind when surfacing, but toothed whales appear to have no sense of smell at all. Dolphins seem able to distinguish between tastes of various fish, and use taste as a form of sexual communication. Recognising the "taste" of different water bodies may also aid in navigation or food-finding.

The bloodshot eye of a southern right whale. Unlike humans, many cetaceans can see well in both air and water.

Anyone touching a live cetacean will marvel at the apparent sensitivity of its skin – even a large whale may shiver at the gentlest

ECHOLOCATION

Toothed whales primarily use sound to hunt. Clicks created within the larynx are focused through the melon, the bulbous fatty organ within the forehead, which functions as a lens. The beam of clicks is used to scan for prey such as fish or squid, or for other solid objects. Echoes returned from a target are probably received through thin windows of bone in either side of the lower jaw and transmitted to each ear. Cetacean echolocation is more sophisticated than any human-made equivalent, such as sonar or ultrasound, allowing target detection as far as 800 m away in optimal conditions. It possibly provides images of richness and complexity that we can only dimly imagine, as we have no comparable sense. There is speculation that intensely focused echolocation can be used to stun prey. So far there is no firm evidence that baleen whales echolocate.

caress. Touch is a major element in social communication, with the intimate contact initiated between mother and calf being carried through into adult interactions in many, if not all, species.

Of the larger species, southern right whales are notably tactile, but touch may not always be gentle in many other species, as is seen in the scarring caused by more aggressive "social" interactions between individuals, particularly mature animals.

Hearing is undoubtedly the primary sense for whales and dolphins. Sound is transmitted in water about four times faster and many times further than in air and, unlike sight, is effective in total darkness. The low-frequency calls of a fin whale, for example, may travel many hundreds of kilometres and can presumably be heard at that distance, but most species' communication occurs over much shorter distances. In a herd of gregarious pilot whales, for example, there is continuous calling as herd members reassure each other of their presence; each animal has a unique, identifying "signature whistle".

The ear bones of cetaceans are separated from the skull and isolated acoustically in a foam-filled cavity. Without sound conduction through the skull, cetaceans can determine the direction of a sound's source by discriminating between signals arriving at each ear. This is a critically important trait. It gives cetaceans the ability to recognise and pinpoint the calls of predators such as orcas, the

In most species, such as southern right whales, cows and young calves are in frequent physical contact. When threatened, calves may "climb" onto their mother's back. As they grow, calves venture farther and farther away from their mothers.

sounds made by prey, or of surf thundering onshore – any of which can mean the difference between life and death.

There is increasing evidence that whales have the ability to detect and navigate by features in the Earth's magnetic field. This might explain some mass strandings where whales have apparently followed magnetic lines of force that crossed coastlines at right angles, yet other strandings show no correlation with magnetic navigation. More research is needed to clarify this.

PREDATORS AND PARASITES

Life in the sea is full of dangers. From the moment of birth, young cetaceans are at risk of being attacked or parasitised by other animals, but their most obvious predators are orcas and sharks. Orcas are fearsome predators – they are intelligent, strong, hunt in coordinated packs, and can tackle anything up to and including blue whales. Their smaller relatives – false killer, pygmy killer and pilot whales – have also been observed harassing or killing other cetacean species on occasion.

The fluke of this humpback whale shows the scarring typical of an attack by orcas, which may "nip" in order to test the vigour of their potential victims.

Contrary to popular myth, sharks are not afraid of dolphins, and may prey heavily on them in certain areas. Great white sharks have been observed harassing and attacking southern right whale calves at Head of Bight, South Australia. Cookie-cutter sharks, less than 1 m long, bite icecream-scoop-sized chunks of blubber 50 millimetres or more in diameter out of whales and dolphins. Even gulls peck at open wounds on the backs of southern right whales, often to the point of driving them frantic. Amazingly, marlin sometimes impale whales, inadvertently snapping off their long, sharp bills after driving them deep into the whales' bodies, perhaps in error while hunting for fish.

External parasites include barnacles and whale "lice", which feed on flaking whale skin and do little harm. Internal parasites, such as flukes and nematode worms, are common and, while some are present in all cetaceans, their numbers can proliferate to the point where an animal's general condition or its navigational senses (if parasites infest the ears) deteriorate to the point of incapacitation or death. Large numbers of such parasites are often found in stranded animals.

BEHAVIOUR

Finding cetaceans is one thing; knowing what they are doing is quite another. Often we may see only a large splash, a group of dolphins rushing past, or a group of whales milling around at the surface. What is going on? Through painstaking observation over many years, researchers have interpreted at least some whale behaviour, much of it concerned with feeding, breeding and social interaction. Although behaviour is complex, subtle and a largely unknown aspect of cetacean biology, the following behaviours are those most likely to be encountered by whale watchers.

AERIAL BEHAVIOURS

These are the most conspicuous and spectacular of behaviours, in which the animal's body, or part of it, projects briefly above the water surface. The most eagerly awaited by whale watchers and photographers alike is the breach, where most or all of the body surges vertically out of the water, landing with a thumping splash. Breaching has a variety of possible purposes: for example, communicating visually or acoustically with other whales; warning boats

A humpback whale mother and calf breach in Hervey Bay, Queensland. As with other animals, young whales learn social behaviours by copying their elders.

Some behaviours often seen in humpback whales (clockwise from top left): lobtailing, spyhopping and flipper-slapping.

that come too close; dislodging irritants such as dead skin, barnacles or remoras; or perhaps it may be an expression of the simple joy of life. Breaching is not to be confused with porpoising: smaller whales, dolphins or porpoises leaping from the water while travelling efficiently at speed. A similar sight, bowriding, occurs when small whales, dolphins or porpoises ride seemingly effortlessly at the head of the pressure wave created by a vessel or a larger whale.

Fluke-slapping (or "lobtailing") and flipper-slapping involve slapping the flukes or flippers loudly on the water and may convey relaxed attention to another whale, perhaps as part of courtship. More vigorous lobtailing may signal annoyance at the approach of a vessel too closely – or it may be directed at another whale, or perhaps at a shark. The slapping of flippers or flukes can be seen and heard for a considerable distance, both above and below the surface. Energetic sideways fluke "slashing" is a defensive tactic whales use when directly threatened, and signifies fear or anger.

When "spyhopping", whales quietly raise their heads vertically from the water. This behaviour is thought to be a method of examining objects above the surface, such as boats. While superficially similar, a "head rise", when the animal's head surges out of the water while it is moving, is a more aggressive gesture.

PHYSICAL CONTACT

Cetaceans frequently touch one another, either gently or roughly. Mothers and young calves spend much of their time gently touching, which reassures both that the other is nearby. As calves age, they treat their mothers more roughly, preparing for the rough-and-tumble of adult social life. Continuous touching, including copulation, is used to affirm social bonds in many species, although at times such interactions appear anything but friendly.

SOUND

Hearing is almost certainly a cetacean's most important sense. Sound is used to maintain contact, mediate social interactions, locate food and express excitement. In the more social toothed whales, there may be a constant "chatter" as individuals affirm their presence, herd food or even squabble. Anyone who has been close to bowriding dolphins may have heard their excited whistles. Humpback whale song can be clearly heard through a hull if the whale is close enough. It is possible, however, to tune into cetacean "conversations" more directly, using hydrophones (underwater microphones), such as the set held by whale researcher, Curt Jenner (right), which enables underwater sounds to be clearly heard.

Touch and sound are the language of cetacean societies, as can be seen in a group of bowriding dolphins, which frequently nuzzle, bump or stroke each other. Anyone who sees southern right whales courting will marvel at the tenderness of their caresses, whereas a competing group of breeding male humpback whales will batter and bloody each other with head-butts and full-blooded blows of flukes or flippers. Most species of toothed whales show some scars from tooth raking and nipping, which are common forms of social discipline and aggression, and may also be part of courtship and mating.

A nervous southern right whale calf sticks close to its mother as she receives unwanted attention from sexually active males. Mothers usually seek to protect their calves from such behaviour.

A blue whale surface-feeding on krill off the Victorian coast. A blue whale may engulf tonnes of water and prey in a single mouthful in its huge throat pouch.

FEEDING

The act of feeding drives much of the social organisation, movements, and behaviour of cetaceans. For example, the group size is largely determined by feeding habits. Many open-ocean dolphins and small toothed whales live in large, coordinated groups with very tight social bonds. Such groups are more effective in hunting scattered, schooling prey over large areas as well as defending themselves against predators. Coastal dolphins that hunt scarcer prey form smaller groups and live in more restricted areas. The larger baleen whales, on the other hand, compete for scattered patches of plankton such as krill and so tend to form very small feeding groups, although these may be stable over many seasons. Some species gulp their food in huge mouthfuls, and others continuously skim it at the surface.

Feeding is often a vigorous, erratic activity, sometimes seen at the surface as rapid splashes, swirls and changes of direction, often with small fish or other prey flying clear of the water. Surface-feeding baleen whales may erupt from below with their cavernous mouths open, often rolling on their sides in order to turn more rapidly through their prey. Much feeding behaviour takes place underwater, sometimes at great depth. All that can be seen of a sperm whale's feeding activity is its flukes hoisted high as it begins its deep dive —

A Bryde's whale feeding on a densely packed anchovy school in Shark Bay, WA. Baleen whales depend on such large schools of fish or crustaceans, eating up to a tonne or more of such food in a single day.

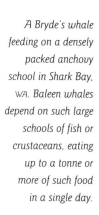

often to more than 1000 m, to pursue its prey. Surface feeding is often indicated by splashing, wheeling seabirds and the bobbing heads of seals and dorsal fins of whales and dolphins as they rush to exploit tightly packed prey.

MIGRATION AND BREEDING

The timing of migration and breeding is driven by seasonal change. Several species migrate regularly each year, some are nomadic and others are more or less sedentary. Many baleen whales exploit the vast swarms of crustaceans, such as krill, copepods and amphipods, in the Southern Ocean during the brief southern summer. After almost doubling their weight, they then migrate to food-poor tropical or temperate waters to breed during winter and spring, when they fast for several months.

Migratory baleen whales gather in their customary breeding areas (the locations of these are still unknown for most species) where complex social interactions regulate the mating of individuals. Calves are born here and return to their area of birth on later migrations, although they may move to other areas later in life.

Many female humpback whales fail to arrive in tropical breeding areas in winter, and many minke whales are seen in Antarctic pack-ice throughout winter, confirming that not all individual baleen

Humpback whales often feed in pairs, which enables them to better herd krill. Expandable throat pleats allow copious amounts of water to be gulped, which is then filtered through their black baleen.

Male humpback whales battle for the right to mate in a warm coral lagoon in New Caledonian waters, about 5000 km away from their Antarctic feeding grounds.

whales migrate each year. Some non-migratory species may breed throughout the year in feeding areas. Of the baleen whales, the warm-water Bryde's whale is the only one to do so. Some oceanic dolphins have breeding peaks in spring and autumn, perhaps in response to a migratory cycle, whereas others breed throughout the year.

Sperm whales have the most unusual migration pattern. Mature males feed in summer in polar waters, while females and young remain in warmer subtropical waters all year round. Males then migrate to join the "nursery schools" in winter to mate and socialise.

Gestation in most cetacean species is 11–12 months, and a calving year is often followed by one or more resting years. In their close-knit societies, toothed whale calves tend to remain with their mother's group for several years, whereas baleen whale calves become independent after the first year of life.

While breeding behaviour is rarely observed in most species, sometimes it is very obvious. Competing male humpbacks form chasing, bruising packs that show little regard for small boats in their vicinity – be aware of the danger!

Most cetaceans are not shy about their sexuality and the act of mating may some-times be easily observed, for example, in southern right whales that mate near the base of the cliffs at Head of Bight, SA. Dolphins often copulate in a social contact that is not necessarily connected with breeding, such as while they are bow-riding. On the other hand, the breeding behaviour of many species is seldom, if ever, observed. For example, very few species have ever been seen giving birth.

MARINE ENVIRONMENTS

Many cetaceans have different habitat requirements at different times of year, particularly those migratory or nomadic species that feed and breed in widely separated areas. Other species live in relatively limited areas in which both feeding and breeding take place. The ecology of cetaceans – their relationship with their environment – is still a developing science, as new methods and technology enable an increased understanding of both the physical environment, and how cetaceans themselves use it for feeding, breeding and travelling.

Breeding requirements are relatively simple, particularly for large baleen whales that fast during the breeding season and therefore do not need food-rich areas for much of the year. Southern right and humpback whales are two such species. They spend the summer feeding in the cold, plankton-rich waters of the Southern Ocean and

Minke whales leading an icebreaker in Antarctic waters. The smallest of the Antarctic baleen whales, minkes are well adapted to these icy conditions, and often remain in these waters year-round.

Humpback whales cruise the placid waters of the Antarctic, which are up to 30° C cooler than their tropical feeding grounds.

the Antarctic, but breed in relatively warm waters along Australia's southern and northern coasts, respectively. Southern right whales seem to prefer shallow, sandy bays near rocky cliffs or headlands, which offer some protection from ocean swell. Much of Australia's southern coast offers these conditions, with the biggest calving area for southern rights at Head of Bight, SA, combining limestone cliffs and long, sandy beaches. This area is not noted for its rich marine life, although it does support resident bottlenose dolphins and sea lions. Southern rights rarely visit NZ now, but a population breeds in protected bays at the subantarctic Auckland and Campbell islands, not far from the whales' Southern Ocean feeding grounds.

Humpbacks prefer fairly shallow, warm water with a flat bottom and protection from swell, often in the form of coral reefs and islands. The Great Barrier Reef off Australia's north-east coast, and the North West Shelf off Western Australia, are major humpback breeding areas, while lesser areas lie inside the coral lagoons of New Caledonia, Fiji and Tonga. Little food is available in these areas. However, on their southward migration after breeding, some humpbacks feed off southern New South Wales and Tasmania, and did so off southern NZ prior to their reduction by whaling.

However, the environment in which large baleen whales feed is far more productive than the breeding environment. Compared to other areas of the world, Australia's continental waters are not very productive biologically. New Zealand's are relatively more so. Phytoplankton, the minute drifting plants that are the basis of the food web, depend on dissolved oxygen, water-borne nutrients and sunlight for growth. In areas where these factors combine, growth is more abundant. Cool southern waters hold more dissolved oxygen than do warm waters, which are generally poorer in oxygen and nutrients.

Oceanic water masses ebb and flow with the seasons, with wind-driven currents bringing major masses into constant contact. Major warm currents flow south along Australia's east and west coasts, and the contact zone, or front, where they meet cooler subantarctic waters is known as the Subtropical Convergence (STC). Such fronts are often areas of intense biological productivity, as cooler, nutrient-rich water is brought to the surface by eddies and mixed with sunlight and oxygen, stimulating the growth of phytoplankton. This is consumed by zooplankton such as krill, and these in turn are eaten by whales, seabirds and fish. Such conditions occur off Tasmania's east coast, and the STC also skirts NZ's southern shores, where humpbacks once fed on krill and crab larvae.

Cool, deep, nutrient-rich water is also brought to the surface by wind-driven currents along the edge of the continental shelf, up submarine canyons or at such isolated features as seamounts. Such upwelling zones, our most heavily productive, are rare in both Australian and NZ waters. Off western Victoria and Rottnest Island, WA, such upwellings attract feeding blue and sei whales. Another

A humpback whale calf swims with its mother in the calm tropical waters of Australia's North West Shelf where it was born. It will soon undertake its first migration across the stormy Southern Ocean to its Antarctic feeding waters.

well-known upwelling occurs off Kaikoura, NZ, where a deep canyon approaches the shore, and sperm whales gather to feed.

Along most of Australia and NZ's coastlines, marine productivity is not high, so cetaceans are rarely abundant, although they live permanently in many areas. Climate, seafloor topography, currents, seawater temperature, and availability of food vary from region to region; coastlines are broken by islands, bays, estuaries, reefs and headlands, and swept by freshwater floods, waves, storms and tides, creating a wide array of aquatic habitats. Hector's dolphins in NZ seem to like areas of freshwater runoff from rivers. Bays or estuaries, such as Jervis Bay and Port Stephens on the NSW coast, have small resident groups of inshore bottlenose dolphins feeding around rocky areas, but many must also forage out along the open coast, maintaining large "home ranges" in order to obtain enough food. Irrawaddy dolphins live in small groups in muddy, brackish tropical rivers and bays. Apart from these small, scattered groups, it is difficult to predict the occurrence of cetaceans. Larger groups of oceanic toothed whales and dolphins rove continually in search of dispersed schools of fish and squid, which may often concentrate along shelf edges, or fronts between water masses.

Throughout their history, cetaceans have adapted to a changing world. They have colonised the oceans from equatorial to polar regions. We don't yet fully understand the complex dynamics of marine environments, and still have much to learn about whales and dolphins. But as our knowledge of them, and of the marine environment, grows, the subtle and intricate links that bind them are becoming more apparent.

The scale of temperature changes in the oceans is shown in these enhanced satellite images of sea-surface temperature. In autumn (top), waters warmed by summer's heat extend southwards, while in spring (bottom), the cooling effects of winter still push colder waters north.

WHALING HISTORY

Whaling and sealing followed hard on the heels of European exploration in Australia and NZ, and were sometimes even the precursors to settlement. Reports of abundant southern right and sperm whales in the Pacific Ocean spurred the arrival of whaling ships from America, Britain and France, with the first ships returning from the "New South Wales fishery" in 1793. The first whaling ships entered NZ waters in 1801, and safe harbours like Sydney and the Bay of Islands became meeting and provisioning places for the growing Pacific Ocean whale "fishery". Sperm whales were sought for spermaceti oil, teeth and occasionally ambergris (until recently used in perfumes), while southern right whales were rich with blubber oil and had long, extremely valuable baleen. In a pre-plastic world, baleen was used wherever a stiff, flexible material was required. Oil had myriad uses, including lubrication, lighting, soap and food products.

The abundance and coastal habits of southern right whales encouraged the development of "bay whaling", in which whalers rowed out to kill whales sighted from land, and then towed them ashore for flensing (cutting up) and boiling down. All whaling during this period was conducted using hand harpoons and lances, from open boats that were launched from ship or shore. It was a hazardous, filthy occupation. Shore stations sprang up along the coasts of NZ and southern Australia, as operators scrambled for their share of riches. There were whaling stations around the southern coasts from Sydney Harbour to Fremantle, and whalers founded such settlements as Portland, Victoria, and Port Lincoln, SA. In NZ, the first stations opened in the mid-1820s in Cook Strait, and later, others dotted the east coast from the top at North Cape to Foveaux Strait at the bottom.

In 1827, when whaling was still a growing industry, there are records of only 64 southern right whales killed in all of south-eastern Australia and NZ combined; by 1839, however, the

The Cheynes Beach Whaling Station, near Albany, WA, where sperm whales killed at sea near the edge of the continental shelf were processed.

industry had boomed and at least 4000 whales were killed (and these are only the ones for which records survive). Southern right whales suffered from uncontrolled exploitation but by 1850, the bubble had burst. In 1860, only 47 southern rights were recorded as taken, and they were rarely seen during the next 120 years: at least 26,000 had been killed, mostly by bay whalers. These records do not include either WA, home to many southern right whales, or the whales taken by many foreign ships that visited Australian and NZ waters, which had no obligation to disclose their catch.

Using sharp-bladed flensing knives, bay whalers strip blubber from a southern right whale on New Zealand's South Island, in about 1860.

Humpback whales were also occasionally taken by bay whalers, as they were almost as slow as southern rights, though far less oil-rich. Nevertheless, with the demise of southern rights, the focus shifted to migrating humpbacks. Some die-hard open-boat whalers carried on their trade into the 20th century: the Davidson family of Twofold Bay, NSW, until 1932; the Te Kaha station in NZ until 1925; on Norfolk Island until the 1950s, and in Tonga up until 1981.

Towards the end of the 19th century, new whaling methods were developed. Whalers from Mr Cook's station at Whangamumu in NZ

A New Zealand whaling station in operation in the 1860s. A whale is cut up (left), the blubber is boiled down into oil (right) and casks of oil (right foreground) are readied to be floated out to a waiting ship.

trapped humpbacks in steel-net traps, then harpooned them from open boats. Then Norwegian whalers introduced fast, powered vessels and explosive harpoon cannons. These methods were adopted by Cook's whalers in 1910, followed by the Perano family of Cook Strait in NZ a year later. In 1912, Norwegian methods were first used to kill humpbacks from Jervis Bay, NSW, and around Shark Bay, WA. The following year sperm whales were also targeted south of Albany, WA. Shore stations that used Norwegian methods later appeared at several Australian locations, such as Tangalooma, Queensland; Byron Bay, NSW; and Carnarvon, WA. These continued their activities into the early 1960s, as did the Peranos and another station at Great Barrier Island, NZ, while sperm whaling at Albany persisted until 1978.

The number of whales killed yearly by these shore stations may by itself have been sustainable indefinitely; the real damage to whale populations was done further south in Antarctic waters. Antarctic whaling began in 1904 at South Georgia in the Atlantic Ocean. By 1930, however, factory ships were operating in the Ross Sea and Antarctic waters south of Australia, the feeding areas of baleen whales that migrate past Australia and NZ. As many as two million whales were killed in Antarctic waters during the 20th century, a harvest that defied commonsense and good scientific advice. One after the other, humpback, blue, fin and sei whale stocks crashed, leaving minkes as the sole species abundant enough to be whaled. The great region of open-ocean whaling extended almost to Australia's shores, with whalers taking pygmy blue and sei whales off the southern and western coasts, and sperm whales around NZ. Apart from "legal" catches reported to the International Whaling Commission, the Soviets (and possibly other nations) operated secretly and without regard for protected areas and seasons, taking mothers with calves as well as critically endangered species, such as blue, humpback and southern right whales.

This onslaught drastically reduced the numbers of whales migrating past our shores to less than five per cent of their former numbers, to the point where sightings became almost non-existent. Whaling became uneconomical and eventually stopped. Even today, the great stream of migrating humpbacks that once passed NZ is no more. However, there is evidence that humpbacks and southern rights, at least, are on the slow path to recovery around Australia's coasts. Other species are not showing such encouraging signs. The Antarctic blue whales, in particular, have barely increased in number in the past 30 years and may never recover from whaling.

THE END OF WHALING

New Zealand ended whaling in 1962, and in 1978 the New Zealand Marine Mammals Protection Act was passed. Humpback whaling from open boats continued in Tonga (right) until 1981, but only a small number were taken each year. The last Australian whaling station, at Albany, WA, closed in 1978, and moral opposition to whaling was adopted and formalised in the Whale Protection Act 1980, *which prohibits the killing or harassing of cetaceans in Australian waters (12–200 nautical miles offshore) and the participation of Australian citizens in killing or harassing cetaceans anywhere. Each State of Australia has since mirrored the Act in legislation that covers State waters (less than 12 nautical miles offshore). Australia and NZ now actively campaign against all whaling.*

CONSERVATION

There were few attempts to conserve whales and dolphins before the 1960s. Most of the large whales were recklessly exploited by whaling, small cetaceans were regarded as insignificant and the deterioration of the marine environment was of little concern. Thanks to many marine scientists, and the efforts of pioneering conservationists such as Rachel Carson, author of *The Sea Around Us*, these issues achieved widespread and growing recognition throughout the 1970s and 1980s, and are now a part of mainstream awareness. Such awareness, however, is only the first step toward resolving most of the problems facing cetaceans.

While whaling constantly threatens to escalate from currently low levels in the Antarctic and elsewhere, it no longer occurs in our immediate region, and should now be regarded as a relatively minor conservation issue globally. Australia and NZ were both whaling nations from the earliest period of European settlement. Both are now prominent in the struggle to conserve cetacean species internationally, largely because opposition to whaling itself crystallised public awareness of other cetacean problems.

To the ends of the Earth: an anti-whaling message posted in the remote Falkland Islands, South Atlantic Ocean.

The oceans themselves have been changed by a range of human activity. One of the most serious is the manufacture and spread of persistent toxic chemicals (notably organochlorines and heavy metals), and the alarming range of conditions they can induce in animals, including cancer, brain damage, suppression of the immune system and reproductive failure. The destruction and alienation of habitats vital to marine species, such as coastal shallows, mangroves, seagrass meadows and coral reefs, continues steadily.

Fish stocks are still mismanaged and overfished. Global warming has the potential to alter the way the ocean's currents circulate which, together with other effects of rising sea temperatures, may radically change marine ecosystems in unpredictable ways. The effects of ozone depletion on increased uv radiation are also of great concern. In addition, the great untapped protein source of krill in the Southern Ocean, vital food for baleen whales, is being eyed by a hungry world.

More real and potential threats have emerged, such as noise pollution in the oceans, offshore mineral development, military testing, entanglement in fishing gear, and disturbance by boats, including some involved in whale watching or research. So far, some of these have been relatively minor, although there is little information about their possible long-term effects.

Other threats, such as driftnet fisheries, have already had catastrophic impacts on marine fauna, including small cetaceans. In northern Australian waters in the mid-1980s, an offshore gill-net fishery was closed by the Australian government to prevent further whale and dolphin deaths. Coastal gill nets have seriously threatened Hector's dolphins in NZ, although steps have been taken to minimise this problem. Toothed whales, such as orcas, are sometimes shot by commercial fishers who consider them a threat to their livelihood, while dolphins are sometimes used for crayfish bait, simply shot for "sport", or run down by boats.

Uncertainty about what actually constitutes a threat is often used to justify the continuation of dubious or dangerous practices. Awaiting conclusive scientific proof that something is going wrong is often courting disaster – science is a slow process and the effects

Driftnets are one of the most insidious threats that cetaceans face. Occasionally discarded, they form imperishable "ghost nets" that continue to entangle marine life for years.

Greenpeace anti-whaling activists harass the Japanese factory ship Nisshin Maru 3 *undertaking whaling operations in Antarctic waters.*

of many problems are subtle and cumulative, and not easily defined until it is too late. At the moment, the burden is on those who seek to protect the environment to prove the connection between a human action and the problem it creates. We would be wiser to adopt the "precautionary principle", wherein those who propose such actions demonstrate that they will not cause harm by proceeding. We are moving in that direction, but slowly.

We are fortunate to live in nations relatively enlightened in their attitudes to conservation, but even so there are many continuing problems and unresolved conflicts. Worldwide, the future for cetaceans is not looking bright, with a multitude of problems taking a huge annual toll. Increasing human population pressure is stripping the sea of its assets. We are running out of time, if we wish to preserve a marine environment that will support itself, and us, into the distant future.

How can we, as individuals, make a difference? You could join a group that campaigns actively for cetacean conservation (some are listed in the Resources section). Such groups are usually under-resourced, and your special skills may be useful. You can write letters of support or protest to government leaders at home or abroad. In your own home and life, you can attempt to minimise your personal contribution to environmental degradation. And each of us can become cetacean ambassadors by talking to our friends, family and workmates about whales and dolphins and their conservation.

RESEARCH

Cetaceans are very difficult animals to study, as they inhabit a medium intrinsically hostile to humans, are often found in remote areas and spend most of their time underwater. Cetacean research (cetology) in Australasian waters commenced in earnest during the 1950s, as an adjunct to humpback whaling. Bill Dawbin in NZ and Graham Chittleborough in WA began a study of life histories and reproductive biology of humpbacks by examining dead whales in whaling stations. This work was later expanded to widespread locations with both men tagging live humpbacks with darts that were recovered when the tagged whales were later killed by whalers. Such data led to an understanding of the humpback migratory cycle. Whaling was the norm at the time, and this research enabled at least some long-term good to come out of whales' deaths. Mainly, it provided the background on which the validity of whaling and loss of stocks was contested, and ultimately (together with the fact that whales had become commercially unviable to hunt) led to the end of whaling.

During the 1970s and 1980s, as the public mood turned against whaling, a revolution occurred in cetacean research. Cetaceans were

Researcher Micheline Jenner painstakingly compares images of humpback whales from WA waters. Photo identification helps researchers learn more about individual whale's movements and life histories.

no longer seen as objects to be exploited, but as fascinating, attractive, wild animals. Pioneering researchers developed new, benign ways to study whales and dolphins without killing them. It was discovered that most species are naturally marked with distinctive, enduring pigment patterns or similarly unique markings, so that photographic identification could replace darting, enabling the study of individual cetacean's lives. The rich world of cetacean underwater sounds was unlocked by the use of hydrophones and detailed studies began to focus on behaviour, and the hitherto ignored details of cetacean societies.

Today, "lethal" research involving the killing of whales or dolphins is illegal and morally condemned in Australia and NZ, although it is still used elsewhere. Benign research ranges enormously in scope: from detailed observations of social relationships in dolphin societies, through to the migratory movements of humpbacks or southern right whales; and from identification of natural markings to the ecological relationship of cetaceans to their environment, which involves studying such complex factors as habitat, oceanography and prey species. Cetacean populations are surveyed from ships, aircraft and headlands to determine their distribution and whether their numbers are increasing or not. Tissue biopsy involves the collection of small samples of skin and blubber from free-swimming animals, in order to determine the genetic structure of populations and species, an important component of conservation biology. Dead stranded animals can be studied to provide a wealth of information on diet, reproduction, parasites and toxic pollution as well as basic anatomy and physiology.

Cutting-edge technology is used in cetacean research in innovative ways. Underwater movements of whales can be plotted by arrays of hydrophones linked to computers; large-scale movements can be tracked by using satellite-linked navigation systems; and video and digital photography create records that

Researcher Tim Edkins samples plankton in a blue whale feeding area off the Victorian coast. Such simple procedures provide valuable data on the whales' diet.

can be transmitted worldwide by email. Researchers are now able to tap into and share an enormous reservoir of information and expertise that was undreamt of a generation ago.

Yet the basis of modern research still requires the simple use of the senses: observation and recording. No matter how sophisticated their technical equipment, researchers must still rely largely on their eyes, ears and intuition to obtain the basic data necessary to understand the lives of whales and dolphins and to analyse the data in a meaningful way.

There is a perception that due to the great breadth of scientific knowledge, we now know most of what there is to know about cetaceans. This is untrue: we have barely scratched the surface. The more we learn about cetaceans, the more questions are raised. We need to understand such basics as: the number of individuals, and even the number of species; what they eat, how they find their food, and how their societies function; how they interpret their environment, and navigate. Most importantly, research must attempt to determine their survival requirements in a changing world, and find ways to secure their future.

Keeping accurate and detailed data is one of the most critical elements in any cetacean research program. Micheline Jenner makes notes of her observations as part of a long-term humpback study along Australia's North West Shelf.

IDENTIFYING WHALES

USING THIS SECTION

This section will help you identify whales, dolphins and porpoises commonly seen in Australian and NZ waters. Each species has a main identification illustration **1** showing its general appearance. This is a scientifically accurate rendering of the species, indicating the shape, prominent features and most common colouration of live animals at sea (once out of the water, whales and dolphins can significantly change colour and shape, so it is important to note that stranded or dead animals can be more difficult to identify; at such times such features as tooth size and number may be diagnostic). The side illustrations **2** show one or more commonly seen features or habits of that species – what you are most likely to see above the waterline. The text gives a brief summary of the most important characteristic features for that species **3**, biology and ecology, and other species for which the species might be mistaken **4**. The Conservation Status **5** at the end of each listing is based on the Action Plan for Australian Cetaceans, which lists existing species in descending order of concern as Endangered, Vulnerable, Insufficiently Known, No Category Assigned or Secure. Most species are listed as Insufficiently Known. There are a number of technical terms, such as flukes, capes, chevrons etc. These are all defined in the Glossary.

The most important diagnostic features **6** are in bold print for quick reference. Often time for observation at sea is very short: to make best use of it, familiarise yourself with the bolded features, and with the figures. Look for key features, such as: estimate of size; shape and size of dorsal fin, and its position on the back; head shape; presence of a beak, or shape of jaws; and overall colour pattern, especially blazes and other distinctive marks and scars. Make notes or sketches as soon as possible after a sighting to help later recall.

As most whale watchers will be on land or on boats near land, the distribution maps **7** show the known occurrence of each species along coastlines, not the complete distribution (it often extends well out to sea but is often unknown or sketchy). So do not discount a species identification if it appears outside its given range.

Not all of the 44 Australasian species are described in full detail here. Rare or virtually unknown species are grouped together at the end under "Other Species". There are 12 species of beaked whales, for example, which are known from the region but are either extremely rarely sighted at sea or, when they are, even experts are uncertain of their identity. So just the two most commonly sighted or stranded beaked whales are included.

SOUTHERN RIGHT WHALE

Eubalaena australis
Family: Balaenidae

- Large, rotund whale that **lacks a dorsal fin**; grows to 17 m
- Large head, curved on top; **lower jaw arched**; no throat pleats
- Pectoral fins broad and paddle-like; flukes often raised
- Body colour usually dark brown to black, with patches of white, often on the belly; some male calves born white and then darken to milk-chocolate brown
- White skin **callosities on jaws and head** arranged in unique patterns, allowing identification of individuals
- 200–270 very long (up to 3 m) grey-black baleen plates
- Bushy, **V-shaped blow.**

Southern right whales breed in shallow bays along the southern coasts of Australia and NZ, and Auckland and Campbell islands. Courtship is relatively gentle – males seldom compete physically for mates and may even cooperate, ensuring they father offspring by producing enormous quantities of sperm that "competes" with other males to fertilise the egg. Females breed every 3 years. Calves are born in winter, weaned 12 months later and return in subsequent years to their calving area. Southern rights mainly feed in the Southern Ocean to about 55°S on tiny crustaceans called copepods, though some feed on krill as far south as the pack-ice edge. Usually found in small groups, aggregations of 100 or more may occur in breeding areas. **Similar Species:** Presence of callosities and lack of a dorsal fin rules out confusion with other species. However, humpbacks sometimes have V-shaped blows. **Conservation Status:** Whaling resulted in only 7000 southern rights remaining from an initial 150.000. Almost extinct by 1850, protected internationally after 1935. Classified as Endangered.

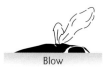

Blow

Flipper

Tail

PYGMY RIGHT WHALE

Caperea marginata
Family: Neobalaenidae

- Streamlined robust whale, grows to 6.5 m
- Hooked dorsal fin, set well back on body; flukes not usually raised when diving
- Upper-body colour dark grey, shading to nearly white on the ventral surface; **no swirling capes and chevrons**
- Small and inconspicuous blow; head may break the surface sometimes when surfacing
- 210–230 yellowish-white baleen plates on either side of the upper jaw; strongly **arched lower jaw.**

Little is known of this inconspicuous whale's life. The smallest baleen whale, it lives only in the Southern Hemisphere at 30–52°S. As strandings occur on Australian shores at all times of year, this indicates extensive migrations are unlikely. Usually alone or in pairs, its social organisation is still a mystery – a gregarious group of 80 was seen recently. Slow, quiet swimmers, they feed on copepod crustaceans and krill but their feeding areas are unknown. They appear to have an extended breeding season, possibly throughout the year, but little else is known of their breeding biology. Calves are about 2 m at birth. **Similar Species:** Minke whale. However, the arched jaw of pygmy rights and their lack of body markings, such as the capes and chevrons found on minkes, should eliminate this possibility. At a distance, confusion with some beaked whales is possible, but up close a beaked whale's bulbous head and narrow snout is visible. **Conservation Status:** The only baleen whale never commercially hunted, perhaps due to its small size and elusive habits. Classified as Insufficiently Known, but this species is probably not rare.

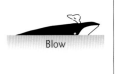

Blow

Dorsal

HUMPBACK WHALE

Megaptera novaeangliae
Family: Balaenopteridae

- Stocky, slow-moving whale, rarely exceeds 15 m
- **Flippers** are a third of body length; variable dorsal fin size and shape; **serrated trailing edge on flukes**, often raised when diving
- **Knobs on top of head**
- Body colour is dark brown to black; often **extensive white pigment** on flippers, flanks and underside of body and flukes; such patterns enable individual recognition
- Bushy blow, occasionally V-shaped
- 270–400 olive baleen plates; 14–35 throat pleats.

Humpback whales belong to the rorqual (groove-throated) family, which includes fin, sei, Bryde's, minke and blue whales. They migrate between their winter tropical breeding areas (Great Barrier Reef, North West Shelf) and summer Antarctic feeding areas. Once common in NZ waters, they are now rarely seen and may migrate further offshore. Males compete for mates either by physical combat or by song. Females calve every 2–3 years; some non-breeding females probably remain in southern waters during winter. Juveniles return to their area of birth but in later life some wander between breeding areas. Humpbacks eat krill and other schooling prey, such as fish, forming small, cooperative groups of 2–3 individuals to feed. They frequently breach, lobtail and spyhop. **Similar Species:** Easily identifiable due to a "hump" back when submerging, but at a distance may be confused with other species that raise their flukes when diving, such as sperm, right and blue whales. **Conservation Status:** Recovering from severe depletion by whaling in Antarctic and coastal waters, they are now at about one-eighth of their former abundance. Classified as Vulnerable.

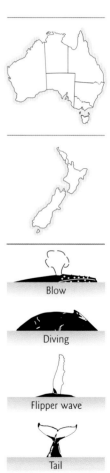

Blow

Diving

Flipper wave

Tail

BLUE WHALE

Balaenoptera musculus
Family: Balaenopteridae

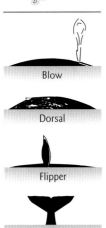

Blow

Dorsal

Flipper

Tail

- **Huge**, slender streamlined whale: "true" blue grows to maximum 33 m (average 25 m); pygmy blue reaches 24 m (average 21–22 m)
- **Very small dorsal fin** located three-quarters of the way down the back; may not appear until the head has submerged
- **Broad, flat head, rounded in front**, with a **prominent central ridge**
- Body colour varies from **light blue-grey to dark grey**, with extensive mottling; appears light blue when submerged
- **Tall dense blow** (up to 9 m), usually at 1–2 minute intervals
- 55–88 throat pleats; 270–400 black baleen plates (up to 1 m in length) on either side of the upper jaw.

Two subspecies of blue whale occur in Australasian waters – the "true" blue, which feeds in Antarctic waters, and the smaller pygmy blue, which feeds in cool waters north of about 50°S. Both subspecies migrate to warm tropical waters to mate and calve. In feeding areas, small groups of one or two whales prey on krill, gulping huge mouthfuls and often rolling onto their sides when surface-feeding. Little is known of their social ecology and behaviour; they rarely breach, lobtail or spyhop. Fast, powerful swimmers, they can reach 37 km/h. **Similar Species:** Fin and sei whales. Blue's great size, colour pattern and dorsal fin shape and position are the main differences. Blue whales raise flukes when diving, and their blow is uniquely powerful. Differentiating true and pygmy blues at sea is extremely difficult, requiring careful estimates of the dorsal fin position. **Conservation Status:** Whaling reduced blue whale numbers from about 220,000 to fewer than 1000. Classification: Endangered. There are perhaps 6000 pygmy blues now compared with 10,000 prior to exploitation. Classified as Insufficiently Known.

FIN WHALE

Balaenoptera physalus
Family: Balaenopteridae

- **Huge, slender, streamlined** whale, can grow to 26 m (av. 22 m)
- **Small dorsal fin** is located **two-thirds along its body** length from the snout, rising at less than 40° from the horizontal, and appears before the head submerges
- Body colour is dark greyish-brown, with pale undersides and pale, **swirling chevron markings** on the dorsal surface behind the head
- Unique **asymmetric lower jaw and baleen colouring**: the left lower jaw and baleen are dark, while the other side is white
- 55–100 throat pleats; 260–470 baleen plates.

The fin whale breeds every 2–3 years in unknown tropical locations. Calves are weaned at 6 months and adults may live as long as 100 years. Little is known of their social organisation, but occasionally they form large aggregations in Southern Ocean feeding areas, taking fish, squid, krill and other crustaceans. They rarely engage in spectacular behaviour such as breaching and are fast, steady travellers. One fin whale covered 3700 km at an average speed of 17 km/h. Like blue whales, they may communicate over long distances using low-frequency sounds, but they also make higher-frequency clicks that could have an echolocation function. **Similar Species:** Blue and sei whales. The blow is markedly less powerful (up to 6 m high) than that of the blue whale (up to 9 m). The dorsal fin is taller than that of the blue whale and intermediate in size and placement between the blue and the sei. This fin is not visible at the same time as the blow. This whale rarely raises its flukes when diving. **Conservation Status:** Reduced by Antarctic whaling to about one-twentieth of their former abundance of about 500,000. Classified as Vulnerable, but it is probably recovering.

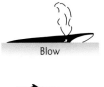

Blow

Dorsal

SEI WHALE

Balaenoptera borealis
Family: Balaenopteridae

- Fast, slender, streamlined whale, to 15–16 m (max. 18 m)
- **Pointed head** (similar to that of a minke whale), with only **one central ridge**
- **Tall, erect, hooked dorsal fin, two-thirds of the way along the body**; flukes rarely raised when diving
- Body colour dark grey or brown, with a **delicate swirling cape** behind the eye; skin may be mottled with **small circular scars**
- Elliptical blow (to 3 m high)
- 32–60 short throat pleats; up to 340 dark baleen plates on either side of the upper jaw.

Sei whales feed in summer through all latitudes of the Southern Ocean, migrating north in winter to breed in unknown warmer waters. They eat fish, squid and krill, but their main prey is smaller crustaceans that they skim-feed at the surface. Seis are shallow divers, so the dorsal fin is visible at the same time as the blow, and may submerge for 15 minutes. Every 2–3 years females bear young – a single calf (4.5 m). Seis are as long as humpbacks but are considerably lighter, weighing 30 tonnes. They are not known for spectacular behaviour, but occasionally breach. Group size is usually fewer than five. **Similar Species:** Fin and Bryde's whales. A sei's dorsal fin is more hooked, and rises at a steeper angle (over 40°) from the back than does a fin whale's. Seis lack the asymmetric pigment pattern found on the head of fin whales. Bryde's whales have three ridges on top of the head. **Conservation Status:** Heavily whaled after the commercial demise of blue and fin whales, seis are still recovering from exploitation. Classified as Vulnerable.

Blow

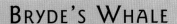

BRYDE'S WHALE

Balaenoptera edeni
Family: Balaenopteridae

- Stocky whale, grows to 14 m
- **Tall, erect dorsal fin two-thirds of the way along the body;** flukes not raised when diving
- **Three ridges** on the head (one median and two lateral)
- Body colour is dark smoky grey; often **covered with circular scars; lacks the swirling markings** seen on the heads of other rorquals
- Tall, thin blow (to 4 m); may exhale underwater (no visible blow).

Bryde's (pronounced brood-ers) is a warm-water whale that does not migrate south of 40°S or into waters cooler than about 20°C. Because this species lacks a seasonal migration, it may breed at any time throughout the year. Females calve every 2 years, bearing a single 3.4 m young, which reaches sexual maturity at about 10 years. Bryde's whales are gulp feeders and consume shoaling fish and invertebrates. When chasing mobile prey, they can suddenly change direction. Bryde's whales form groups of 10–20 in feeding areas, but little else is known of their social organisation. **Similar Species:** Sei whales. However, at close range the three rostral ridges are a distinctive diagnostic feature and Bryde's has a stockier body. Seis also dive deeper and rarely show their flukes. Whales sighted south of 40°S are unlikely to be Bryde's. **Conservation Status:** While the population status of Bryde's is unknown, it is thought to be secure from any threat of extinction. Classified as Insufficiently Known.

Blow

Surfacing

Top of head

MINKE WHALE

Balaenoptera acutorostrata
Family: Balaenopteridae

- **Small whale**, grows to 10 m (dwarf form, 7 m)
- **Sharply pointed head**, with **prominent median ridge** in front of blowhole. Line of mouth is straight, not bowed
- **Tall, sickle-shaped dorsal fin, two-thirds down the body**
- Body colour is dark slatey grey, with pale to white undersides
- **Inconspicuous blow**, except in very cold weather
- 30–70 throat pleats; 230–360 grey-white baleen plates.

Two forms of minke whales inhabit Australasian waters. The "dark shoulder" form is larger, with a prominent light-grey flank patch, a pale "cape" behind the head and a grey flare on the dorsal fin. It summers in Antarctic waters, feeding on krill, but elsewhere may feed on other crustaceans and fish. Winters are spent either in sea-ice or in tropical breeding areas. The "dwarf" form (illustrated top) is found in warmer waters, has a less prominent flank patch, a grey-white scimitar-shaped mark above the flipper, and a darker dorsal fin. It may be seen in coastal waters May–December, with 80 per cent of sightings in June–July. Both types of minkes can breed every year; calves are only about 2.8 m at birth. Group size is usually small, with dwarf minkes most often being solitary or in pairs, but they may form groups of up to eight. Renowned "ship seekers", both types often approach slow-moving or stationary vessels. They create large splashes when surfacing at speed. **Similar Species:** Sei, Bryde's, some beaked whales, and can also be confused with pygmy right whales. Their pointed heads, straight jaw and distinctive pigmentation distinguish them. **Conservation Status:** The dark-shoulder form is abundant, occurring in Antarctic waters in hundreds of thousands. Classified as Secure (dwarf is Insufficiently Known).

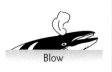

Blow

Dorsal

SPERM WHALE

Physeter macrocephalus
Family: Physeteridae

- Large whale that grows to 18 m (females 12 m); **huge, squarish head, heavily wrinkled skin** over middle half of body
- Body colour is black to brownish-grey; white patches around mouth and on belly
- **Raised dorsal hump** and prominent "knuckles" along ridge of tail
- Blowhole at front left side; **blow angles distinctly forward and to the left**; blows repeatedly while resting, then dives vertically with flukes raised to feed
- Raised blowhole and dorsal hump may appear to be two animals
- Long, narrow **underslung lower jaw** holding 36–50 large teeth in lower jaw only.

Sperm whales dive deep – up to 3 km – to feed on squid and fish along continental shelf edges, seamounts and other areas of upwelling. They are only seen close to land where deep water approaches the coast, such as at Kaikoura, NZ. Some dives exceed 2 hours. During summer mature males feed in Antarctic waters singly or in pairs, while females and young remain in "nursery schools" of 10–50 in warmer waters. Young males form bachelor herds that decrease in size with age. Older males are usually solitary and visit nursery schools for mating during winter. Hundreds of sperm whales may travel together at the surface. They use low-frequency clicks for communication and echolocation. **Similar Species:** At a distance, humpbacks may appear similar, particularly when diving, but the sperm whale's blow is unique – it blows continuously (tens of times) before diving. **Conservation Status:** Once heavily whaled but now protected and still relatively abundant. Classified as Insufficiently Known.

Blow

Diving

Tail

PYGMY AND DWARF SPERM WHALES

Kogia breviceps and *Kogia simus*
Family: Kogiidae

- **Small, slow, inconspicuous** whales that grow to 3.4 m (in the pygmy, the species illustrated) and 2.7 m (in the dwarf)
- **Dwarf has a larger dorsal fin** near the middle of the back; **pygmy has a smaller more rounded fin** in the same position
- Body colour is dark grey on the back with a whitish belly; "**false gill" mark** behind the eye
- Both have a **blunt, almost shark-like head**, with a narrow under-slung lower jaw; pygmy has squarer head
- Teeth: pygmy has 12–16 on each side of the lower jaw; dwarf has 8–13 on each side of the lower jaw, and up to 3 on each side of the upper jaw
- Inconspicuous blow.

These two species are little known and only studied during strandings and rare sightings at sea. Both are difficult to detect: they rest low in the water, and "drop" into it when submerging. Mainly squid eaters, they occur along continental slopes in warm temperate to tropical zones. No migrations are known. When disturbed, they may emit a cloud of faeces, possibly as an escape screen. Group size appears to be small, and is usually no more than five or six. Little is known of their social lives or their reproductive biology, although calving may occur in summer. **Similar Species:** These two species are almost impossible to differentiate at sea, other than on dorsal fin height: in the dwarf it is 5 per cent of body length and in the pygmy, 3 per cent. **Conservation Status:** Nothing is known of the population status of these species. Some are killed in gill nets in the Indian Ocean, but no immediate threats have been identified in Australian and NZ waters. Classified as Insufficiently Known.

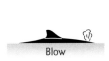

Blow

Blow

ORCA (KILLER WHALE)

Orcinus orca
Family: Delphinidae

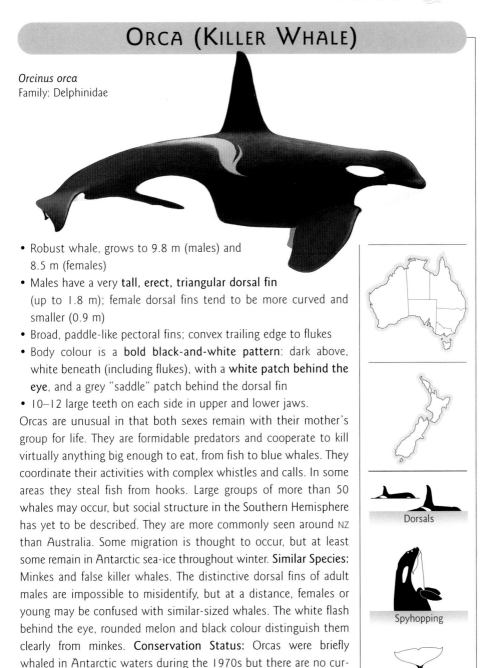

- Robust whale, grows to 9.8 m (males) and 8.5 m (females)
- Males have a very **tall, erect, triangular dorsal fin** (up to 1.8 m); female dorsal fins tend to be more curved and smaller (0.9 m)
- Broad, paddle-like pectoral fins; convex trailing edge to flukes
- Body colour is a **bold black-and-white pattern**: dark above, white beneath (including flukes), with a **white patch behind the eye**, and a grey "saddle" patch behind the dorsal fin
- 10–12 large teeth on each side in upper and lower jaws.

Orcas are unusual in that both sexes remain with their mother's group for life. They are formidable predators and cooperate to kill virtually anything big enough to eat, from fish to blue whales. They coordinate their activities with complex whistles and calls. In some areas they steal fish from hooks. Large groups of more than 50 whales may occur, but social structure in the Southern Hemisphere has yet to be described. They are more commonly seen around NZ than Australia. Some migration is thought to occur, but at least some remain in Antarctic sea-ice throughout winter. **Similar Species:** Minkes and false killer whales. The distinctive dorsal fins of adult males are impossible to misidentify, but at a distance, females or young may be confused with similar-sized whales. The white flash behind the eye, rounded melon and black colour distinguish them clearly from minkes. **Conservation Status:** Orcas were briefly whaled in Antarctic waters during the 1970s but there are no current direct threats to their survival. Classified as Insufficiently Known, but they are undoubtedly common and widespread.

Dorsals

Spyhopping

Tail

FALSE KILLER WHALE

Pseudorca crassidens
Family: Delphinidae

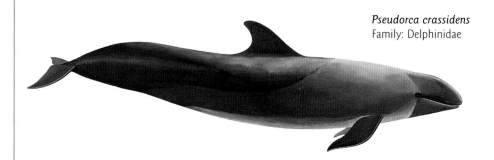

- Long, slender whale, grows to 6 m (males) and 5 m (females)
- **Tall, slender, hooked dorsal fin** in the middle of the back
- Flippers are set well forward on the body, and have a **distinct "elbow" and a sickle-shaped leading edge**
- Body colour is dark grey to black, with a light-grey chest patch
- Long, tapered **head often comes well clear of the water** when surfacing
- 7–12 teeth on each side of upper and lower jaws.

False killer whales are members of the blackfish family, which includes orcas and pilot whales. Often called pseudorcas, they are distributed widely in warmer waters but are not common. They eat squid and fish, preferring deeper waters along continental shelf edges and may mass strand when they pursue prey closer inshore. However, they have often been sighted in shallow water around northern Australia. Most strandings occur in winter, indicating possible seasonal migrations. They often approach boats and will raid longlines for fish, and may occasionally attack and tear pieces off larger whales. Fast and acrobatic, false killer whales often breach, and travel in pods of about 50, though larger groups may form temporarily. Breeding occurs all year round, but there may be long intervals between calves, which measure up to 1.8 m at birth. **Similar Species:** Pygmy killer and melon-headed whales. The false killer whale is larger than either of these whales and has distinct "elbows" in the sickle-shaped flippers. The pygmy killer whale has a rounded head. **Conservation Status:** No immediate threats in Australasian waters. Classified as Insufficiently Known, but it is probably Secure.

Surfacing

Dorsal

PYGMY KILLER WHALE

Feresa attenuata
Family: Delphinidae

- Smallest "whale"; grows to 2.6 m with a **rounded head**
- **Flipper tips rounded** rather than pointed
- Tall dorsal fin
- Body colour is grey, grey-brown or blue-black, with a dark dorsal cape, **white lips** and a white belly patch; has a distinctive whitish-grey blaze along sides of the chest and flanks
- 8–12 teeth on each side of the upper jaw; 10–13 on each side of the lower jaw.

Pygmy killer whales are similar in many respects to melon-headed whales. While essentially a warm-water species, a few have stranded as far south as the north coast of NSW. Their diet includes fish and squid but they have also been seen to herd and kill dolphins, both in the wild and while in captivity. They are more sedate swimmers than melon-headed whales and are sometimes seen swimming in line abreast. They are regarded as aggressive and may snap and growl if closely approached, although they generally avoid boats. Group size is usually fewer than 50. Nothing is known of their breeding biology or if they migrate. **Similar Species:** Melon-headed whales. The pygmy killer whale has a more rounded head, more rounded flippers and its dorsal cape dips less than that of the melon-headed whale. **Conservation Status:** There are incidental catches in gill nets but this species is thought to be uncommon in Australasian waters. Classified as Insufficiently Known.

Surfacing

Dorsals

SHORT-FINNED PILOT WHALE

Globicephala macrorhynchus
Family: Delphinidae

- Stocky whale with a **large, bulbous forehead**; grows to 6.1 m (males) and 5.5 m (females)
- **Low, rounded, broad-based dorsal fin** set well forward
- **Flippers are about one-seventh of body length** (shorter than those of long-finned pilot whales)
- Body colour is dark grey-brown to black, with **pale-grey saddle**; grey streaks behind the eye; white ventral patch
- 7–10 pointed teeth on each side of upper and lower jaws
- Blow is small and indistinct.

Nicknamed "potheads" by whalers, after the shape of the head, short-finned pilot whales inhabit waters warmer than 22°C. They live in stable family groups of up to 50, which interbreed, and live for at least 63 years. Short-finned pilot whales have calving peaks in spring and autumn, calving every 4–6 years. Older females act as "wet nurses" for younger females' calves, during their post-reproductive period. Unfamiliarity with shallow waters may cause the frequent mass strandings that occur in these deep-diving squid eaters. They often accompany other whale and dolphin species, and have been seen attacking sperm whales. They probably move around in response to prey movements. **Similar Species:** Long-finned pilot whales occur in colder waters; otherwise the two species are impossible to differentiate at sea. False killer whales have different head and dorsal fin shapes. **Conservation Status:** Pilot whales are still whaled around Japan, but there are no current direct threats in our region. Classified as Insufficiently Known, but this species is probably Secure.

Blow

Fin

LONG-FINNED PILOT WHALE

Globicephala melas
Family: Delphinidae

- Stocky whale with a **large, bulbous forehead**; grows to 6.7 m (males) and 5.7 m (females)
- **Low, rounded, broad-based dorsal** fin set well forward
- **Very long, tapered flippers** (about one-fifth of body length)
- Body colour is dark grey-brown to black, with **pale-grey saddle**; grey streaks behind the eye; white ventral patch
- 8–12 pointed teeth on each side of upper and lower jaws
- Blow is small and indistinct.

Long-finned pilot whales live in very stable family groups of up to 50 and sometimes gather into aggregations of 1000 or more where food is plentiful. Individuals communicate with bird-like chirps. Long-finned pilot whales are deep-diving squid and fish eaters, although they are sometimes seen near coastlines, and may mass strand. Older females act as "wet nurses" for younger females' calves, after their own reproductive life has ended, and this species may live more than 63 years. They have calving peaks in spring and autumn, and calve every 4–6 years. They usually lie or move quietly at the surface but are also known to breach, porpoise and spyhop. Found in cool to cold water (1–20°C), penetrating south almost to the edge of the sea-ice, and often seen in the company of other species. **Similar Species:** Short-finned pilot whales. While it is almost impossible to distinguish the two at sea, their ranges rarely overlap with short-finned pilot whales occurring in waters warmer than about 22°C. **Conservation Status:** There are no current direct threats in Australia and NZ, although oceanic heavy metal and organochlorine contaminations are of concern. Classified as Insufficiently Known, but probably Secure.

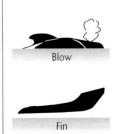

Blow

Fin

MELON-HEADED WHALE

Peponocephala electra
Family: Delphinidae

- Slender, elongated, small whale with a **tapering, pointed head**; grows to 2.7 m
- Tall, slightly hooked dorsal fin with rounded tip
- **Long, flippers, pointed at the tip**, one-fifth of body length
- Body colour is blue-black, brown or grey; **whitish lips; black face "mask"**; dark cape dipping below the dorsal fin
- Often avoids boats, but may bowride on occasion
- 20–25 teeth on each side of upper and lower jaws.

Also known as electra dolphins, melon-headed whales are fast swimmers that often porpoise while travelling at speed. They are generally found in waters warmer than 25°C, where they feed on squid and small fish. The herd size of these gregarious animals varies from fewer than 40 to more than 2000, and they have been involved in mass strandings on the east Australian coast, but are not known to migrate. They are not yet confirmed in NZ waters. They often associate with other species and have been observed possibly attacking other dolphins. They may mate in spring, and 1-metre-long calves are born 12 months later. **Similar Species:** Pygmy and false killer whales. Pygmy killer whales are very similar, but have a more rounded head, shorter flippers with a rounded tip, and lack the dorsal cape of the melon-headed whale. While false killer whales may appear similar at a distance, they are much larger. **Conservation Status:** Very common in the eastern tropical Pacific and around the Philippines, melon-headed whales may also be common in Australasian waters. Classified as Insufficiently Known.

Spyhopping

Leaping

STRAP-TOOTHED BEAKED WHALE

Mesoplodon layardii
Family: Ziphiidae

- Slender whale; grows to 6.2 m
- Adult males have a **large, distinctive flattened tusk**, halfway along each lower jaw, that meet over the upper jaw
- Small hooked or triangular dorsal fin; small flippers that broaden toward the tip before rapidly tapering; triangular **flukes, not notched** in the centre
- Body colour is predominantly black, with a **large white patch extending along the top** of the back from the dorsal fin to the back of the head and around to the chin and throat; black face; white ventral patch in the genital region
- Inconspicuous blow.

Strap-toothed whales are one of the most commonly stranded beaked whales in both NZ and in the cooler regions of Australia, but they are very rarely sighted at sea. They are shy of boats, and can dive with barely a ripple. The function of the remarkable teeth of males, which prevent the jaws from fully opening, is a mystery; teeth of females do not erupt at all. Like other beaked whales, they dive deep to feed on squid, which they probably capture by intense suction. Many individuals are covered with linear scars that are probably caused by tooth raking from members of their own species. Group size is usually fewer than three. Calving occurs in spring and summer. They are not known to migrate. **Similar Species:** Other beaked whales. If close enough, the curved teeth of adult males will be distinctive. **Conservation Status:** No current threats are known in Australasian waters, although entanglement in gill nets and exploitation of squid resources may have long-term effects. Classified as Insufficiently Known.

Surfacing

GRAY'S BEAKED WHALE

Mesoplodon grayi
Family: Ziphiidae

- Slender whale reaching 5.6 m in length
- **Small, hooked dorsal fin**, and flippers that broaden toward the tip; **flukes not notched**
- Upper body colour is **dark blue-grey to black**, paling towards the underside, which is pale grey, often with light spots; white linear tooth scars are common
- **Small triangular tooth** at centred lower jaw of mature males
- Small head and flat forehead; **long white beak** with a straight mouthline; sometimes lifted above the surface.

This species, also known as Scamperdown's beaked whale, occurs south of 30°S. Little is known of its biology, although these whales strand relatively frequently, especially in NZ, where nearly 100 different strandings have been recorded since 1873. They may be fairly social, as indicated by one stranding involving 28 animals. At sea they are sighted more frequently than most other beaked whale species, perhaps due to their habits of breaching, porpoising and poking their heads above the water when surfacing. They eat squid and fish, possibly caught at depth. It is not known whether they migrate and their breeding biology is unknown. **Similar Species:** Other beaked whales. However, the long white beak is very distinctive. **Conservation Status:** This species may be vulnerable to set nets and large-scale exploitation of squid. Classified as Insufficiently Known.

Surfacing

BOTTLENOSE DOLPHIN

Tursiops truncatus
Family: Delphinidae

- **Large, robust dolphin** that matures at 2–3.5 m
- **Stocky beak** separated from the forehead by a well-defined crease
- **Tall, hooked dorsal** fin in the middle of the back
- Body colour ranges from almost black to light grey on the back and sides, and white or pink on the undersides; faint dorsal cape, visible at close range; many tooth rakes may be present on the skin
- 18–28 large teeth on each side of upper and lower jaws.

A familiar species, bottlenose dolphins are found from estuaries and bays to the deep waters of the open sea. There are two "forms" in Australasian waters – the larger, darker offshore form, which may be migratory, and the better-known smaller, paler inshore form, often spotted ventrally in adults, which has resident populations at Monkey Mia in WA, Bay of Islands in NZ, and Jervis Bay in NSW. These forms may prove to be separate species. Daily activity patterns involve feeding around rocky areas where fish and other prey are common, resting and socialising. Females calve every 2–3 years. Group membership changes frequently but core groups of males or females persist. Bottlenose dolphins are inquisitive and active, frequently bowriding, jumping, breaching and surfing. **Similar Species:** Common, spinner, rough-toothed and humpbacked dolphins. However, if seen closely enough, bottlenose dolphins are usually quite distinctive, with the form of the beak and body shape usually enabling a clear identification. **Conservation Status:** Threats include habitat destruction, entanglement in set nets, overfishing of prey species and pollution – especially for the inshore form. Classified as Insufficiently Known, but it is widespread in Australian and NZ waters.

Surfacing

Spyhopping

Leaping

INDO-PACIFIC HUMPBACKED DOLPHIN

Sousa chinensis
Family: Delphinidae

- Robust dolphin that grows to 2.8 m, with a long, slender, well-defined beak below a moderate melon
- Low, **rounded, triangular dorsal fin** in the middle of the back
- **Distinctive surfacing behaviour:** the beak or entire head breaks the water surface at an angle of 30–45°, the back arches strongly, and flukes often raised when diving
- Calves are very pale grey, becoming dark grey above and paler underneath with age before lightening in colour and developing dark spots on the sides and belly
- 26–38 teeth on each side of upper and lower jaws.

This species lives inshore in tropical to subtropical waters between Shark Bay, WA, and the Queensland border, although a stranding has occurred as far south as Wollongong, NSW. They may live further from land within the Great Barrier Reef and other shallow areas. Groups of fewer than 10 patrol channels, bays and rocky headlands searching for fish. They also eat crustaceans, squid and octopus, and may follow prawn trawlers for discarded fish, Between breaths they tend to remain below the surface. However, active surface behaviours have been noted, such as breaching, jumping (including somersaults), fluke slaps and head slaps. Breeding probably occurs all year round, with a peak in summer. Maximum lifespan is at least 40 years. **Similar Species:** Bottlenose dolphins. The Indo-Pacific humpbacked dolphin has a lower, rounded dorsal fin and distinctive surfacing behaviour. **Conservation Status:** Trapped in gill nets in northern waters. Loss or modification of habitat, such as mangroves, is also a concern. Classified as Insufficiently Known.

Surfacing

Dorsal

Diving

SPINNER DOLPHIN

Stenella longirostris
Family: Delphinidae

- **Slender dolphin** with a **long, narrow beak**; grows to 2.4 m
- **Dorsal fin is tall and hooked** (may be more erect in older males); flukes only slightly notched
- Flippers long, curved and tapering to a point
- Body colour is grey without spotting; dark dorsal cape; light-grey sides; whiter underside; may be a dark streak from eye to flipper
- 45–65 small sharp teeth on each side of upper and lower jaws.

A mainly tropical dolphin, this species has been reported as far south as Bunbury in WA. Not often seen around the Australian coast, they do enter the Gulf of Carpentaria; there are no reports yet from NZ. Herd size may be from 15 to several thousand. They are extremely agile, getting their name from their habit of spinning on their long axis during high leaps, and they are ready and nimble bowriders. Unlike many other dolphin species, they are thought to bottom-feed on reef fish, squid and crustaceans in depths to 200 m. Their gestation period is thought to be 11 months, and they live up to 20 years but little else is known of their breeding biology. **Similar Species:** Bottlenose or common dolphins. The beak is noticeably more slender than that of bottlenose dolphins, while the dorsal cape is not V-shaped below the dorsal fin, as seen in common dolphins. **Conservation Status:** Formerly comprised about one-third of the kill in gill nets in northern Australian waters until 1986, and may still be vulnerable to gill nets set outside Commonwealth waters. Classified as Insufficiently Known, but probably very abundant.

Spinning

Porpoising

STRIPED DOLPHIN

Stenella coeruleoalba
Family: Delphinidae

- Slender dolphin with a medium-length beak; grows to 2.6 m
- Hooked dorsal fin
- Body colour is dark grey on the back, light grey on the sides, and white on the underside; appendages are dark; **distinctive dark stripes** run from the eye to the anus, and from the eye to the flipper; pale-grey blaze extends backwards into the dorsal cape toward the dorsal fin; small dark streak behind the eye
- 40–55 small sharp teeth on each side of upper and lower jaws.

The striped dolphin is mainly a warm-water species, reaching Augusta in WA, and the north coast of NSW. It has also been reported around NZ's North Island during summer. A fast swimmer, it is acrobatic above the surface, and bowrides, but may be more flighty than other species. Striped dolphins eat a variety of squid and fish and some crustaceans that congregate along the continental slope. They are not found close to the coast where the continental shelf is wide, such as in Australia's north. Herds usually number in the low hundreds, although thousands sometimes assemble. Australian breeding peaks are unknown but around Japan they occur in summer and winter, and schools segregate on the basis of sex and age. **Similar Species:** Spotted, spinner and common dolphins. All these species are similar in shape and size, but the body markings are distinctive. Fraser's dolphin is more robust, the flank stripe is much broader and the fins and flukes are proportionally much smaller. **Conservation Status:** Exploited elsewhere by purse seine and "drive" fisheries, striped dolphins may be taken in gill nets in Australia's northern waters. Classified as Insufficiently Known, but it is still common.

Porpoising

COMMON DOLPHINS

Delphinus delphis and
Delphinus capensis
Family: Delphinidae

- Slender, streamlined dolphins with a slender beak; to 2.6 m
- Tall dorsal fin
- Distinctive **"hourglass" pattern on flanks**, the front half of which is tan or yellow, the back half grey, highlighted above by the dark cape and below by the pale belly; flippers, flukes and dorsal fin grey to black; complex facial colour pattern, with a dark circle around the eye, a dark beak, and a **thin black streak from the mid-length of the mouth** to the pectoral fin.
- Up to 60 small, pointed teeth in each side of the upper and lower jaws (more than any other cetacean).

Common dolphins vary considerably worldwide, but it is now clear that there are at least two species – the short-beaked common dolphin (*D. delphis*), illustrated above, which lives both inshore and offshore, and its coastal relative, the long-beaked common dolphin (*D. capensis*). They are very difficult to differentiate at sea. The presence and distribution of both species in the region is being researched. They move in search of fish and squid, sometimes forming huge herds of several thousand individuals, and may undertake seasonal migrations. There can be much splashing as animals surface in synchronised groups, and they are keen bowriders, sometimes staying with a vessel for hours, when their whistles may be easily heard. Aerial behaviours such as breaching, porpoising and lobtailing are often seen. Breeding can occur all year round and the calves are nursed for about 18 months. **Similar Species:** Spinner or bottlenose dolphins. However, at close range the colour pattern of common dolphins is unmistakable. **Conservation Status:** Classified as Insufficiently Known, although undoubtedly common.

Porpoising

FRASER'S DOLPHIN

Lagenodelphis hosei
Family: Delphinidae

- Stocky dolphin that grows to 2.7 m
- **Very small flippers and flukes**
- Pointed dorsal fin
- **Very short beak**
- Dorsal body colour is dark greyish-brown (almost black at times), with a **broad lateral stripe** (more prominent in older animals) that runs from the apex of the melon through the eye and along the flank to the anus (darkens to black with age); narrow dark band runs forward from the flipper to the middle of the mouth; white or pink belly and throat
- Often forms large herds, with energetic swimming creating much white water
- 33–44 teeth each side of upper and lower jaws.

This little-known species was first recorded in the wild only in 1970. They are usually found in warm deep water toward the Equator, but warm ocean currents have brought occasional vagrant sightings or strandings as far south as Corio Bay, Victoria. They are often seen in mixed schools with other toothed whales, and feed on fish, squid and crustaceans. Little is known of their social organisation or breeding biology, although they may form herds of thousands on occasion. They usually avoid boats, rushing away at speed in tight groups, but are known to bowride in some areas. **Similar Species:** Striped dolphin. These may appear similar at a distance, but Fraser's is more robust and has a shorter snout than the striped dolphin. Can also be confused with bowriding bottlenose dolphins. **Conservation Status:** Classified as Insufficiently Known.

Porpoising

ROUGH-TOOTHED DOLPHIN

Steno bredanensis
Family: Delphinidae

- A streamlined, robust dolphin that grows to 2.8 m
- Large, tall, hooked dorsal fin
- Flippers curved and rounded at the tip
- Large eyes; **long, conical beak, with no demarcation from melon**
- Body colour is dark grey, with **narrow, dark dorsal cape** (especially in front of the dorsal fin); white on the lips, lower jaw and belly
- Often covered with **tooth rakes and cookie-cutter shark bites**
- 20–27 teeth on each side of upper and lower jaws.

Rough-toothed dolphins prefer deep offshore waters warmer than about 25°C, where they feed on fish and squid. Sometimes lethargic, they may be seen logging at the surface, but may also move fast with their heads raised above the water – a swimming style known as surfing or skimming. They also porpoise and bowride, and often associate with other small cetaceans. They are usually seen in groups of fewer than 20, but nothing is known of their breeding biology. They occur around northern Australia; there are no reported sightings from NZ. **Similar Species:** Bottlenose dolphins. The form of the head or the dorsal cape readily distinguishes the rough-toothed from the bottlenose dolphin. **Conservation Status:** Classified as Insufficiently Known.

Logging

Skimming

IRRAWADDY DOLPHIN

Orcaella brevirostris
Family: Delphinidae

- A slender dolphin that grows to 2.7 m
- **Blunt head with no beak**, on a flexible neck; straight mouthline
- Small, triangular, slightly hooked **dorsal fin with blunt tip**
- Long, broad, curved flippers with pointed ends
- Body colour is **blue-grey to brownish** on upper surface and almost white on the underside
- **Inconspicuous swimmer** with invisible blow
- 15–20 teeth on each side in upper and lower jaws.

Irrawaddy dolphins inhabit shallow inshore tropical and subtropical waters throughout South-East Asia and northern Australia from North West Cape, WA, to Gladstone, Queensland. They often enter rivers and mangrove-lined bays. They are slow-moving animals that roll smoothly when surfacing, and often raise their flukes when deep diving. They feed on fish, squid and octopus, and crustaceans such as prawns. Group size is normally fewer than six and no more than 15; they are sometimes solitary and they hold individual territories. Occasionally they indulge in active behaviour such as breaching, lobtailing and porpoising, and when spyhopping they sometimes spit water from their mouths. Breeding probably occurs in spring or summer, after a 14-month gestation, and they may live up to 30 years. **Similar Species:** Dugongs, and bottlenose and humpbacked dolphins. Dugongs lack a dorsal fin, while the other dolphin species have a distinct beak and larger dorsal fin. **Conservation Status:** Irrawaddy dolphins sometimes drown in gill nets in northern Australian waters. In other parts of Asia, habitat modification is of such serious concern that there are fears Australia will become the last stronghold for the species. Classified as Insufficiently Known.

Dorsal

Diving

RISSO'S DOLPHIN

Grampus griseus
Family: Delphinidae

- **Large, robust dolphin** noticeably more slender behind the dorsal fin; grows to 3.8 m
- **Head is blunt, with a bulging forehead and no beak**; vertical crease down the front of the melon
- Dorsal fin is **curved and very tall**; flippers are long and pointed
- Body colour is **grey to almost white**, with a pale underside; often **covered with tooth rakes and scars** that increase in extent with age; appendages are darker than the body
- 2–7 pairs of teeth in the front lower jaw, and none in the upper jaw.

Risso's dolphins prefer warmer water and are rarely sighted in Australasian waters, although there have been occasional sightings off Fraser Island, Queensland, and some other States. The famous dolphin Pelorus Jack that "guided" ships in the Marlborough Sounds in NZ early this century was a Risso's. They may calve throughout the year, after a 13–14 month gestation. Primarily squid eaters, they gather along continental shelf edges to feed, usually forming small groups but occasionally herds of hundreds. They sometimes swim side by side, possibly to help locate food. Spyhopping, lobtailing, surfing and other active behaviours are sometimes seen. They associate with other species. A few rare hybrids with bottlenose dolphins have been recorded. **Similar Species:** False killer whales, orcas and bottlenose dolphins. At a distance they may be confused with other large dolphins with a tall dorsal fin, but the grey body and extensive scarring become obvious when close. **Conservation Status:** They are thought to be reasonably abundant, but are caught in gill nets in Asian waters. Classified as Insufficiently Known.

Surfacing

Spyhopping

Dusky Dolphin

Lagenorhynchus obscurus
Family: Delphinidae

- **Small, robust dolphin** with a very short beak; grows to 2.1 m
- Dorsal fin is tall and hooked, two-tone (dark with a lighter trailing edge)
- Curved flippers are grey with a dark trailing edge
- **Complex body colour**, with dark grey to black above, and white below; broad grey patch running back from the face, tapering towards the belly; dark beak; **grey blaze on the hind part of the body that forks forward below the dorsal fin**
- 27–36 small pointed teeth on each side of upper and lower jaws.

Dusky dolphins usually live close to coastlines and islands in the cooler temperate waters of the Southern Hemisphere. They are fairly common south of East Cape, NZ, to Campbell Island and are often seen by whale watchers at Kaikoura. In Australia, confirmed sightings have occurred only since 1986, near Kangaroo Island, SA, and on Tasmania's east coast, and are possibly rare instances of migration. Duskies are gregarious animals and may form herds of thousands but usually feed cooperatively in smaller groups of 15 or more, eating small fish and squid. Very acrobatic, they are well known for their tumbling leaps, and bowride readily. Calving occurs in midwinter, when animals are generally further offshore than in summer. **Similar Species:** If seen closely enough, the distinctive colour pattern of dusky dolphins should avoid confusion with any other dolphins. **Conservation Status:** Relatively abundant worldwide, many are drowned in gill nets in NZ. Classified as Insufficiently Known.

Porpoising

Leaping

HECTOR'S DOLPHIN

Cephalorhynchus hectori
Family: Delphinidae

- **Very small**, robust dolphin that grows to 1.5 m
- **Small, well-rounded dorsal fin**
- **Blunt head** lacking a distinct beak
- Body colour is **light grey**, with dark grey to black dorsal fin, flippers, flukes, face and blowhole; white underside, with extensions reaching up the sides
- 26–32 pointed teeth on each side of upper and lower jaws.

Hector's dolphins are found only in NZ coastal waters. They are non-migratory and often reside in localised areas. There are three separate populations – on the west and east coasts of the South Island, and the west coast of the North Island. They are often found in murky water near river mouths, where they eat fish, crustaceans and squid. This species usually lives in small groups of 2–12, but on occasion as many as 60 animals may gather, when they may leap, spyhop, chase and "pounce" (where one dolphin jumps on top of another). They are generally sedate, and while they often accompany slow boats they rarely bowride. They also surf in rough weather. Unusually for dolphins, they do not whistle, communicating only in rapid high-frequency clicks. They calve in spring and early summer; the tiny calves weigh about 9 kg. **Similar Species:** The small size, uniquely shaped dorsal fin and distinctive colouring make this species difficult to confuse with any other. **Conservation Status:** Hector's dolphins are rare, with a total population of 3000–4000 individuals. A sanctuary has been established around Banks Peninsula to protect them from gill nets. Classified as Endangered.

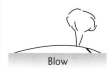
Blow

Dorsal

Leaping

SOUTHERN RIGHT WHALE DOLPHIN

Lissodelphis peronii
Family: Delphinidae

- **Long, slender dolphin** that grows to 2.5, possibly 3 m
- **No dorsal fin**
- Small white flippers may have dark leading or trailing edge
- A strikingly marked dolphin, **black above and white below**, with white extending to the beak, and a sharp demarcation line along the flanks
- 44–49 sharp, pointed teeth on each side of upper and lower jaw
- **"Bouncing" swimming motion**; frequently leaping clear of the water when moving fast in groups.

A distinctively patterned cetacean, the southern right whale dolphin is a cool-water species living in the deep water of the Southern Ocean, where it eats squid and small fish such as lantern-fish. These dolphins may form groups of more than 1000 animals, or fewer than 30, and are often noticed by the whitewater commotion they make as they porpoise along in synchronised groups. In NZ waters they are rarely sighted, although strandings have occurred between Foveaux Strait and Northland. In Australia, they have been sighted off Tasmania and in the Great Australian Bight. Their remote, deepwater habitat makes them difficult to study, consequently little is known of their biology, ecology or behaviour. **Similar Species:** Lacking a dorsal fin and having such a unique coloration make this species impossible to confuse with any other, although at a distance they may be mistaken for penguins. **Conservation Status:** No known threats exist for this species. Classified as Insufficiently Known.

Porpoising

OTHER SPECIES

The remaining 14 species found in Australian and NZ waters include more beaked whales, rarely seen dolphins, and one porpoise, which has only rarely stranded on Australia's southern shores. In most cases, too little is known to create identification illustrations.

•**Shepherd's beaked whale:** Known only from rare strandings, mostly in NZ, this beaked whale reaches 7.1 m. Live animals have never been seen. *Tasmacetus shepherdi.*

•**Arnoux's beaked whale:** The largest Southern Hemisphere beaked whale, it reaches 9.6 m. While sighted in Antarctic waters in large gregarious groups, it may breed in tropical waters. *Berardius arnuxii.*

•**Longman's beaked whale:** Known only from two skulls: one from Queensland and the other from Somalia. Length estimated at 7–8 m. *Mesoplodon pacificus.*

•**Blainville's beaked whale:** This species occasionally strands on warm and cool Australian shores, but is not known from NZ. A dark-grey beaked whale, it reaches about 5.8 m. *Mesoplodon densirostris.*

•**Hector's beaked whale:** This small beaked whale grows to about 4.5 m. It has stranded in NZ, Tasmania and SA, but living animals have been seen off California, indicating a broad distribution. *Mesoplodon hectori.*

•**Andrew's beaked whale:** Strandings have occurred in NZ, southern Australia, and Macquarie and Campbell islands in the Southern Ocean. Dark blue-black with a white beak, this species may reach 4.5 m. *Mesoplodon bowdoini.*

•**True's beaked whale:** Occasional strandings are known from southern Australia but no living specimens have been seen. Length may attain 5.3 m. *Mesoplodon mirus.*

•**Gingko-toothed beaked whale:** Two have stranded in NSW and one in the Chatham Islands, NZ. A uniform blue-black, it reaches about 4.8 m. Teeth of males are shaped like a gingko leaf, which resembles a giant maidenhair fern. *Mesoplodon gingkodens.*

•**Cuvier's beaked whale:** Strandings have occurred all around NZ and Australia, with reports of live animals in mid-Southern Ocean. Schools of up to 25 have been seen. Length may reach 7 m. *Ziphius cavirostris.*

•**Southern bottlenose whale:** Probably one of the deepest divers of all whales. Strandings have occurred in southern Australia and NZ, and the species is reported to be common in Antarctic waters in summer. Estimated 7–8 m. *Hyperoodon planifrons.*

•**Hourglass dolphin:** A strikingly marked small dolphin (to about 1.8 m), common in Southern Ocean waters as far south as the sea-ice edge. May bowride in schools of up to 100. *Lagenorhynchus cruciger.*

•**Pantropical spotted dolphin:** Large schools of this species have been sighted off NZ, and strandings are known from warmer parts of Australia. The only spotted dolphin in this region, it may reach 2.2 m in length. *Stenella attenuata.*

•**Spectacled porpoise:** A subantarctic species reaching about 2.2 m. It has stranded in Tasmania and subantarctic islands; live animals have been seen in small groups south of NZ. *Australophocoena dioptrica.*

WATCHING WHALES

WHY WATCH WHALES?

Whether it's the quicksilver vitality of bowriding dolphins or the power and grace of a great whale breaching, watching whales in the wild allows us to connect with the awesome excitement of our natural world. Whale watching encompasses many activities, from joining a commercial vessel for a cruise, to paddling a sea kayak near dolphins, or even sitting quietly on a headland observing the ocean. For many people, the first experience of viewing a whale in the wild is an unforgettable revelation. But whale watching is more than a passing spectacle, and serious whale watchers are aware that understanding whales and appreciating their problems is a crucial factor. It can be easy to harm or harass whales inadvertently so that they no longer frequent favoured whale-watching locations.

In choosing a whale-watching cruise, it is worth seeking out an operation that has a knowledgeable naturalist or researcher on board. He or she will provide background information about the whales' natural history and ecology, interpret behaviour, and gather

Whale watching in all its forms can provide some intensely memorable experiences. Here, two boys interact with dolphins at Monkey Mia, WA, where whale watching is now a prime tourist attraction.

useful scientific information. After such a cruise, a whale watcher can return not only with vivid memories of living whales, but also with a greater understanding of them.

Boats are not the only means for seeking whales. Land-based whale watching is greatly underrated: it is leisurely, free, gives a greater sense of animals moving through their environment and, most important, has no impact on the whales. While humpbacks and bottlenose dolphins are still the major focus for boat-based operations, humpbacks on migration are also commonly seen from headlands, and it is a delight to discover dolphins leaping in the surf. Southern right whales are best viewed from cliffs and headlands in breeding areas. How you observe them will often depend on the location, and on the species you are interested in. Both techniques give quite different experiences, each offering unique insights into whales, dolphins and their environment. Usually they do not exist in the same area: boat-based whale watching is not desirable in areas where good shore-based watching is possible, as the presence of boats can often alter the behaviour of the whales, one of the great attractions of land-based watching.

Whale watching is largely about curiosity and co-existence between remarkably different animals.

Cliffs at Head of Bight, SA, where the southern right whale calves, a top spot for land-based observing.

THE WHALE-WATCHING INDUSTRY

Whale watching is not always profit-driven. Earthwatch volunteers work in a happy partnership with researchers and crew on Whalesong, *a research vessel. They will help collect and collate data and the fees they pay for the voyage help fund the research program.*

Whale watching in Australia has mainly centred on three of the more predictable species: bottlenose dolphins, humpback whales and southern right whales. While best known as a modern boat-based industry, whale watching as a recreational activity probably originated at Monkey Mia in WA, where in the 1960s bottlenose dolphins gathered inshore at a remote fishing camp to accept fish from fishermen. The boat-based industry arose in 1987, and focused on humpbacks stopping in Hervey Bay, Queensland, on their south-ward migration from breeding waters.

Commercial whale watching also began in NZ that year, at Kaikoura on the South Island, and whales now attract 70,000 visitors a year to this town. The main species of interest is the sperm whale, which was whaled in this area briefly in the mid-1960s, but orcas, pilot whales and dusky and Hector's dolphins are also commonly seen.

Whale watching is now a significant industry, with a direct value of nearly A$10 million in Australia in 1995, and an estimated value of NZ$15 million in NZ. There are presently more than 150 companies operating in Australia, and 74 current whale- and dolphin-watching licences in NZ, with the numbers continuing to grow.

WHALE WATCHING FROM LAND

While some cetacean species live most of their lives out of sight of land, others inhabit coastal waters or estuaries, or regularly migrate past coastlines, and are easily seen from suitable lookouts. Residents of coastal areas may be unaware that whales or dolphins occur in their "backyards", yet land-based whale watching can offer some of the most rewarding encounters.

There are several advantages to land-based watching. For a start, all the hassles of organising a boat are bypassed: you simply make your way to a good lookout and stay as long as you like. There are hundreds of locations, usually free, from those better-known ones such as Cape Byron and Victor Harbor in Australia or the clifftops in Kaikoura in NZ, to a multitude of ordinary headlands. Most importantly, land-based whale watching has no impact on the whales:

KEEPING RECORDS

Keeping a record of your sightings has several useful purposes: it helps you to recall details later and to notice patterns, or unusual events or behaviour; it trains you to observe more carefully; and it may be useful to researchers – there is every chance that you may see something unusual. Handwritten notes and sketches are the simplest and most common forms of record-keeping, although tape recorders, photography and, particularly, video are also extremely valuable.

Sometimes a species can be identified only with hindsight, so note, sketch, film or photograph distinctive features if you can, during or soon after the sighting. Not only does this help you to learn to identify a species, it also means you will be able to confirm your identification.

Try to record the following:
- *The species (if known) and reasons for your identification.*
- *Identifying features (if species unknown), in particular, the body length, colour pattern, shape of the head and snout and, if present, the position and shape of the dorsal fin.*
- *Distinctive scars, pigmentation and other marks (sketch or photograph if possible).*
- *The approximate number and size of animals, and whether calves are present.*
- *Behaviour, such as breaching, feeding, porpoising or resting.*
- *Any other wildlife present, for example, fish schools, seabirds, seals, sharks.*
- *Weather and sea conditions, and whether any boats are present.*

There is a blank logbook page on the last page of this book you can copy for making your own records. If you want to make observations that could be useful to cetacean researchers, contact your local wildlife authority for advice. Contact details are provided in the Resources section.

they are free to engage in their natural behaviour, completely oblivious to your presence, without the effects that the presence and noise of vessels or aircraft may have on them. One negative effect that has emerged in some locations, however, is degradation of coastal landforms and vegetation by large numbers of whale watchers. Try to minimise your own impact on these often fragile environments.

In order to find a good land-based whale-watching site, consider both the vantage point and the likelihood that cetaceans will be present. It's necessary to gain only a little height to greatly increase the distance over which you can scan, and the higher the better. Lighthouses, which occupy high, commanding positions, are usually excellent. Headlands and cliffs are usually worth a look, as whales often pass close inshore.

When you go whale watching along the coast, be well equipped. There's no point going in bad weather, as the condition of the sea will prevent you from seeing whales. But at other times you may need protection from wind, sun and heat or cold as extended periods exposed to the elements can take their toll on the unprepared, especially as most whale-watching activity takes place during winter months. A pair of binoculars or a spotting telescope is essential to bring those distant splashes or the faint puffs of blows into focus as living animals.

A southern right whale swims off the NSW south coast near Ulladulla. Their preference for breeding in bays makes them a likely species for shore-based whale watchers to spot.

Potentially good sites are of little use, however, if whales or dolphins are not in the area. Some coasts are rarely visited by migratory species, while migrants such as humpbacks regularly pass some coasts, but only at certain times of year. Southern right whales visit their coastal breeding areas only during winter and spring. In many areas, however, resident species, such as bottlenose, dusky or humpbacked dolphins, may be found throughout the year. When you choose to visit an area, try to ascertain beforehand what species may be present. During the humpback migration along the coast of NSW, for example, with patience you are almost certain to see whales.

Work out your own technique – either with the naked eye or with binoculars – for scanning slowly and systematically around the sweep of ocean, not forgetting to check in close as well as out to the horizon. Anything unusual is worth investigating – splashes or swirls, fleeting dark shapes, flocks of feeding birds, something that disappears and reappears suddenly, anything resembling a blow. Remember that cetaceans are usually on the move, so try not to make the common mistake of focusing on the spot where they dived, as they will usually resurface some distance ahead of this point. Some whales may submerge for 10 minutes or more.

Patience is the greatest asset in land-based whale watching: as with fishing, the rewards come to those who are prepared to put in a little time, to slow down to the pace of the sea and its creatures. Even if you do not see cetaceans every time, you will start to notice other things – surface schools of fish, migrating flocks of birds, the movements of fishing boats – all pieces in the intricate jigsaw of the marine environment, of which cetaceans are an indivisible part.

Early on a cold July morning in Coffs Harbour, these whale researchers have risen to catch the blows of whales highlighted by the rising sun. Spotting whales is not always easy, but experience helps, as does commitment.

SWIMMING WITH WHALES

Swimming with cetaceans is allowed in a few locations in Australia and NZ (in particular, Port Phillip Bay in Victoria, and the Bay of Islands and Kaikoura in NZ), despite guidelines advising against it because of the risk of injury to swimmers. In Queensland, stringent regulations prohibit swimmers entering the water within 300 m of cetaceans, three times the distance boats are allowed to approach.

Your desire to swim with the animals may not be shared by them and you may disturb their natural behaviour, with unpredictable consequences ranging from flight to aggression. Even small dolphins are powerful animals, and swimmers have been seriously injured or killed by them. So, don't jump in with a group of feeding, resting or aggressively interacting whales or dolphins, don't intrude on their space, and never attempt to climb onto their back. Mothers with calves are particularly sensitive to disturbance, and one may react violently if she feels that her calf is threatened. Cetaceans need to be quietly approached to no closer than the minimum permitted

distance. Then it is up to them to choose to approach swimmers or not, and they may need to be given the space to leave if they wish. Scuba gear is inadvisable, as many species use underwater bubble clouds as a threat: your exhaled bubbles may be interpreted as such.

On the other hand, swimming with animals that welcome the interaction can be an amazing experience. In what appears to be a unique situation worldwide, dwarf minke whales regularly approach snorkellers and divers at the Ribbon Reefs near Cairns, Queensland, initiating and maintaining contact sometimes for hours, often within a few metres.

This southern right whale has been approached by a swimmer, who is careful to make no attempt to get any closer than the whale will allow him.

FEEDING WHALES

Feeding of cetaceans is not permitted anywhere in NZ. In Australia, feeding of dolphins is illegal in Queensland, and highly discouraged elsewhere. Bottlenose dolphins are fed in only three highly regulated situations: Monkey Mia and Bunbury in WA, and Tangalooma in Queensland. Various concerns have been raised, however, including disease transmission, dolphins becoming dependent on handouts, changes in social behaviour and reduced wariness of humans, in some cases leading to aggression.

At Monkey Mia, recently fed adult males were able to devote much more time to harassing females, possibly contributing to calf mortality. New restrictions there include not feeding males, allowing young to be more or less independent before they are hand fed, and reduced levels of feeding: hopefully these measures will

Though it may be well-meaning, feeding wild dolphins can lead to their dependence on handouts and becoming too familiar with humans.

enable feeding to continue there without significant impact. You may be tempted to feed dolphins that approach your boat, but it is better not to do so. For the reasons stated, it's not a good idea to train wildlife to expect handouts from passing vessels.

WHALE WATCHING FROM SEA

In Australia, the steady increase of humpback populations on both the east and west coasts has led to a proliferation of boat-based commercial whale-watching operators. Dolphin watching has also become an important boat-based industry in some areas.

One of the great joys of whale watching is to be approached by a curious whale, which may spyhop, swim underneath your boat or simply lie alongside. In a small boat, this can be an unnerving experience. However, usually whales are extremely aware of boats, and will be gentle around them. They will physically attack only when extremely threatened and as a last resort. Sometimes, an inquisitive or playful whale may rub, bump or push your boat. Do not panic: either wait and see what happens next (the whale may often satisfy its curiosity and move away), or start the engine and retreat as quietly as possible, taking care not to engage the propellers while the

Bottlenose dolphins approach a boat in Shark Bay, WA. The whale watcher has cut the motor and allowed the dolphins to investigate him.

whale is underneath your boat. You may injure or at least alarm it.

Boating around whales has inherent dangers. If you are unfamiliar with boats, take at least one experienced boat handler. Make sure the boat carries adequate safety equipment (as required by law), especially if you are going onto the open ocean. Consider the conditions, and check weather forecasts. Don't wait until you are forced to seek shelter: the sea makes no allowances for the unprepared.

Boats and aircraft can easily disturb cetaceans if certain etiquette is not observed and approach distances are not respected. Private boat owners need to familiarise themselves with the guidelines and disturbance behaviours, not only for the whales' sake, but also because they themselves may be at risk, especially in small boats. Disturbed behaviour is not difficult to recognise (see page 79) and yet even some commercial operators seem to be unaware of it, and may pursue or harass whales that are displaying their displeasure by breaching, lobtailing or mock charging. There is no excuse for commercial operators being unaware of these signs and, if in doubt, they should back off. If you feel any boat operators are overstepping the

BOATING TIPS

• *Will you be at sea, or in protected waters? If at sea, take precautions for seasickness, as nothing can ruin an outing more thoroughly than being sick. Do not drink alcohol or have a big meal before leaving.*

• *Take suitable clothing. Wind, rain and cold are merely inconveniences if you're properly equipped. If not, they can make life utterly miserable.*

• *Take a hat, sunglasses, sunblock and protective clothes. Sunlight reflected off water can burn fiercely, and in places you have never been burnt before.*

• *Remember that boats are not always stable platforms. Move around them carefully, always with a hand free to steady yourself.*

• *Take your camera or video. Use fast film (200 ASA or faster) with a shutter speed of 1/500 or faster to freeze the movement of cetaceans, as both they and the boat may be moving. A telephoto lens (100–300 mm) can produce great close-ups. Take a waterproof cover for your equipment (a plastic bag will do) in case of rain or saltwater spray.*

A humpback whale inspects a research yacht in WA waters. Sailing vessels are preferred by researchers because their silence under sail means the whales are more likely to approach the vessel.

limits, question their behaviour and, if warranted, report inappropriate behaviour to the relevant government wildlife agency.

Vessels with noisy outboard engines, hovercraft and jet skis should never be used for whale watching. Sailing vessels are ideal – they are quieter and cause less disturbance to the whales.

WHALE WATCHING FROM THE AIR

Aircraft can offer unparalleled views of cetaceans at sea as it is possible to see over a wide area and follow the animals after they have dived. Aircraft are commonly used for cetacean surveys, and in some areas, for whale watching. But aircraft can affect cetaceans with their sudden appearance, engine noise, the shadow they cast and, in the case of helicopters, rotor wash. Cetaceans can react by switching from resting or social behaviour into rapid swimming, turns, dives or shorter surfacing periods. Helicopters, in particular, can provoke fright reactions such as diving and breaching.

Minimum altitudes apply for all aircraft flying near cetaceans. In most areas, this is 300 m within a 300 m horizontal radius of a cetacean. Circling, overflying and causing your shadow to pass over cetaceans are strongly discouraged, and "buzzing" them is illegal and something quite distressing for the animals. Leave the animals alone if they change direction, speed or diving behaviour once you have arrived. In Australia, helicopters may soon be banned from commercial whale watching, but any helicopter flying over the sea will frequently encounter cetaceans – they need to maintain a distance of at least 400 m horizontally and vertically as they pass.

THE ETHICS OF WHALE WATCHING

Every time someone steps onto a boat, an aircraft or gets into the water to see whales, it is essential to remember that whale watching is essentially exploiting a precious, possibly fragile, resource. Despite the end of whaling, whales are under pressure from many other threats. Worldwide, the marine environment is steadily being degraded, and many human activities threaten whales directly – habitat destruction, overfishing, pollution (ranging from lost drift nets to pesticides), fisheries "bycatch", ship strikes, ocean noise etc. As a consequence, many species such as humpbacks and southern right whales are at a fraction of their former numbers, and are still on the precarious path of recovery.

At the same time, whale watching has become an economic lifeline to many seaside communities: it has provided a comparatively benign alternative to whaling by making whales the resource for another multi-million dollar industry. But as this relatively new industry is based on the free-swimming wild existence of these animals, it is vital to ensure it does not threaten their lives and wellbeing. The industry as a whole has yet to develop and operate in such a way.

For all its economic benefits, the long-term effects of whale watching on cetaceans are yet to be determined so, to avoid unforeseeable problems, a precautionary approach is essential.

When whaler Ben Boyd built his tower south of Eden, NSW, in 1847, whaling was a profitable industry. Today the same tower and Boyd's Inn earn money for the region as prime tourist attractions.

But the difficulties are obvious. Migrating humpback whales, for example, are now subjected to the physical presence of boats and the resulting engine and propeller noise along huge stretches of Australia's east and west coasts, often by vessels whose operators are not aware of the whales' needs. Many of these are commercial whale-watching boats, perhaps run by fishing or dive operators alert to new opportunities. The industry cannot operate purely by market forces as these usually ignore biological realities. In order to minimise the harmful effects on the whales, a permit process is necessary to regulate the number of licensed operators carrying out commercial whale watching, one that requires them to behave in specified ways. However, in several Australian States there is no such permit system, leaving regulation of the industry to market forces.

Another concern with commercial whale watching is that great emphasis is put on sightings. Beware such expectations – whales are not very predictable. A useful alternative for operators is to present whale and dolphin ecology tours, in which cetaceans are but one component, along with weather, seabirds, currents and fisheries. Sightings are thus given a meaningful framework and, if there are no whales seen, customers still have a deeper appreciation of the whales' world, and a satisfying natural history experience nonetheless, better preparing them for their next attempt to find whales.

Unless each commercial whale-watching trip acts with sensitivity to whales' needs and includes a concerted effort on the part of the operators to inform and educate the passengers, then such activities merely put the target cetaceans at risk from disturbance, displacement, harassment and collision with no potential long-term benefits for them. When such education is provided by commercial operators it adds value to their trips and also helps create advocates for cetaceans, empathy for their wellbeing and an understanding of their environment and all its complexities.

It is indisputable that humans benefit from whale watching – personally, commercially and even spiritually. The best outcome of "enlightened" whale watching would be the full recovery of endangered species and an understanding and appreciation of their lives.

Spectators watching southern right whales at the viewing platform at Logans Beach, Warrnambool, in Victoria. Purpose-built platforms such as this one offer unobstructed viewing and they minimise erosion of the fragile clifftop environment.

GUIDELINES AND REGULATIONS

While most commercial operators behave responsibly and respect the whales' needs, some do not. Whales and dolphins are generally tolerant and apparently good-natured animals, but as they increasingly become the focus of human interest, it is necessary to regulate the activities of humans around them, not only to protect the animals from harm and disturbance, but also to protect zealous whale watchers from harm by whales. As it is logistically impossible for wildlife authorities to monitor and enforce whale watching in all areas, the industry must be largely self-regulating. This requires a responsible and restrained approach by operators, remembering that these animals are their livelihood.

Dolphins and whales often seek out boats and stay with them for extended periods, as here at Althorp Island, off Yorke Peninsula, SA. It should always be the cetacean that chooses whether or not to continue with such interactions.

Permit systems, where they exist, regulate operator numbers and require them to abide by guidelines (and in some cases, regulations). These guidelines and regulations, on the other hand, have been established to regulate the behaviour of all vessels, not just those of commercial operators. We must consider the huge potential impact of other vessels, such as recreational fishing boats, whose operators are largely ignorant of cetaceans and their needs – partly because they have not been required to be otherwise. Perhaps education programs could be tied to ordinary boating licence requirements, to minimise disturbance from this source.

Disturbance can take two main forms – physical and acoustic. Vessels can physically intrude on whales' space by crowding too close, surrounding them or separating individual animals. Vulnerable animals such as mothers and young calves are more sensitive to such perceived threats, and can react with desperate and dangerous attempts to get past the offending vessel: two people died on a Mexican whale-watching vessel when a gray whale was separated from its calf by the boat. Acoustic disturbance can interfere with whales' normal communication, or simply annoy them, at surprisingly great distances. Cetaceans live in a sea of sound, and unwelcome sounds can disturb them as much as any

DISTURBANCE BEHAVIOURS

When disturbed by boats, aircraft or swimmers, whales often (but not always) change their behaviour in one or more of the following ways:

- *Fluke slashing (right), fluke slapping (below), breaching, head rises or other vigorous surface behaviours.*
- *Frequent changes in speed or direction, usually away from the disturbance.*
- *Loud growling blows, underwater bubble blowing or other loud underwater noises.*
- *Increased breathing rate indicated by increased blow frequency or stronger blows.*
- *Prolonged diving with changes of direction while underwater, often away from a boat.*
- *Change from a quiet state to other behaviours, such as those listed here.*
- *Mock charges at the boat, sometimes with throat inflated, and with audible growls.*

Such behaviours may not always be a response to your presence. Whales respond to the presence of other whales or predators such as sharks. Discretion and commonsense is required to determine whether the whales are reacting to you or to something else. If you are unsure, assume that you are the cause of the disturbance and move away to a reasonable distance.

physical harassment. Whales will turn to avoid the underwater noise of vessels several kilometres away. Aircraft can cause underwater as well as above-water noise, and their physical presence, especially helicopters, can disturb or intimidate whales.

The fact that whales and dolphins may remain in a locality while they are being subjected to close attention does not necessarily mean that they are indifferent to it. Animals engaged in vital activities such as feeding, courting and mating, may be very reluctant to leave areas where these activities have been carried out for millennia. They may tolerate intense whale-watching pressure only because they have no alternative. On the other hand, whales are clearly not bothered by the presence of boats in many whale-watching areas, and are either indifferent to them or seek them out.

All Australian States as well as the Commonwealth of Australia,

WHALE-WATCHING GUIDELINES

Minimum approach distances	NZ	AUST **	TAS	VIC	NSW	QLD	WA	SA
Boats	50 m* whales only	100 m	100 m	150 m* motor vessels	100 m	100 m*	100 m	100 m*
Swimmers	100 m* whales only	30 m	30 m	30 m	30 m	300 m	30 m	300 m*
Aircraft	150 m	300 m*	300 m*	300 m*	300 m*	300 m*	300 m*	300 m*
Limit on number of vessels <300 m	3	3	3	–	–	3	–	–
Feeding permitted?	No	No	No	–	–	No*	No*	–

NB *Whale watching is not a recognised activity in the Northern Territory, and there are no provisions for regulating it.* * *Special conditions apply – seek more information from your local wildlife authorities.* ** *Commonwealth of Australia (national) guidelines.*

have whale-watching guidelines and these are currently under review in order to iron out inconsistencies between them. There are legal regulations only in NSW and Queensland. In NZ, the *Marine Mammals Protection Regulations 1992* are in place.

Such guidelines set out minimum approach distances, the speed and manner in which boats should approach, leave and behave around cetaceans, the need to assess the response of cetaceans to human presence, and the appropriateness or otherwise of certain human activities (such as feeding or swimming with cetaceans). These guidelines are not, however, based on the biological realities of the whales' world. If they were, approach limits might, in some circumstances, be set at several kilometres, the distance at which some whales have been observed to avoid the noise of approaching vessels. Guidelines are a compromise between giving the close viewing that the industry wants and attempting to minimise the effects of such close approaches; they also provide a mechanism for dealing with offenders, under various laws. There are grey areas. There is a difference between boats approaching cetaceans and the reverse. Many cetacean species regularly approach boats well within the allowed limits – for instance to bowride – and there are no minimum

Given space and consideration, whales will often seek close encounters. Here a humpback mother and calf swim under a whale-watching vessel in Hervey Bay. Such interactions may continue for considerable periods.

HOW TO APPROACH CETACEANS

It is a good idea to plan how you will act when you encounter cetaceans. You may come across them unexpectedly, or you may be looking for them. Keep in mind the following "rules":
- *Do not approach cetaceans head on or directly from behind, or place yourself directly in their path; either wait quietly ahead and to one side, or approach from behind and to one side.*
- *When within 300 m, gradually slow to a "no-wake" speed, with no sudden changes in direction, speed or engine noise. Allow the engine to idle both before switching off and after switching on.*
- *Never separate animals in a pod, especially mothers and calves.*
- *Never pursue a cetacean that apparently avoids you or shows disturbance behaviours.*
- *Never herd or drive cetaceans.*
- *Sit quietly at a distance, rather than attempting to get too close. Whales and dolphins will often approach a quiet vessel that gives them space.*
- *If a whale approaches you, slow down and allow your engine to idle in neutral, before switching off. If you don't want a close encounter, move away slowly.*
- *Always keep a good lookout and, if there are whales about, slow down to avoid collisions.*

The speed and agility of dolphins means that they will always call the shots during a bowriding encounter.

approach distances for dolphin watching in NSW for this reason. Obviously, cetaceans are free to choose to accompany a vessel, and this is a desirable and wonderful thing. However, this is not the same as placing yourself in among a group of migrating whales, which have no choice but to proceed in their chosen direction, although they may resent your company.

This brings us to the critical matter of harassment: what is it, how do we recognise it and how can we avoid it? Harassment can be defined as persisting in approaching or following whales or dolphins, after they have shown avoidance or disturbed or altered behaviour. Such short-term effects of disturbance may be subtle, but with practice, can be readily recognised. The possible long-term effects of disturbance on cetaceans are of great concern, such as abandoning favoured areas, reduced ability of mothers to care for their young, changes in mating or feeding behaviour, or increased mortality through a combination of these and other effects.

STRANDINGS

One of the most perplexing and saddening aspects of cetacean behaviours is the tendency to strand. It is not entirely understood how such wonderfully adapted marine animals come to be in such a helpless situation, washing around in surf, being pounded on rocks, or slowly dying on a beach, their blowholes choked with sand. "Dead strandings" are easily explained: an animal dies at sea, and is driven ashore by wind and tide. But how do living animals, with their acute senses and their mastery of the water, allow themselves to be removed from the element that sustains and protects them? That they often strand in groups is even more puzzling. Is it deliberate, or have they somehow lost their way?

A wide range of species is known to strand alive, from the largest whales to some of the smallest dolphins. Strandings vary from individuals to herds numbering hundreds, but some interesting patterns have emerged. Species that often approach land, such as humpbacks and southern right whales, rarely strand; when they do so, they are usually alone. Pilot, false killer and sperm whales, which strand most often and in great numbers, live most of their lives in

This scene depicts the worst of all stranding scenarios – a mass stranding of very large whales, whose size makes them virtually impossible to rescue. This stranding of 100 sperm whales took place near Strahan on Tasmania's west coast early in 1998.

Sometimes strandings call for unusual practices. A group of melon-headed whales that stranded at Point Plomer, NSW, in 1996, were temporarily transferred to a motel swimming pool to stabilise them until they could be relocated to sheltered waters for rehabilitation before their release. Suncream has been applied to avoid their skin becoming sunburnt.

deep water away from coastlines and form large, cohesive social groups.

It is possible that disease or parasitic infection can cause whales to approach the shore, either through disorientation caused by parasites in their ears, which are important for navigation, or a desire to gain an extra few hours of life. Another possibility is that deepwater species may approach the shore in search of prey. When they do, they move into unfamiliar territory, full of dangers. Sandbars, falling tides, headlands, heavy surf, and a gently shallowing bottom that does not reflect echolocation signals – all can contribute to disorientation. Another theory is that some cetaceans are sensitive to fluctuations in the Earth's magnetic field, which they use for navigation, and that anomalies in these force-fields may deceive them. In a stranding of more than 100 sperm whales in Tasmania in 1998, the first whales ashore were seen to make a bee-line for the beach, as if they were travelling somewhere beyond it.

Why do whales mass strand and why do they rejoin their companions on the beach after they have been returned to the water? In highly social species, the key lies in their tight group bonds. These gregarious whales constantly depend on each other for cooperation with feeding and for protection. If one of them is stricken with disease or swims ashore through navigational error, the others will not abandon it. Stranded animals issue distress calls to their companions. When returned to the sea, whales will often restrand themselves, but this makes sense when we realise that their mother, calf or other close companions are still ashore.

HOW TO DEAL WITH STRANDINGS

You may have the misfortune to be first on the scene of a stranding. While strandings present unique opportunities to examine cetaceans at close quarters, they can also be overwhelming in that there is often nothing to be done for the stranded animals. Large whales are particularly daunting, as it is usually physically impossible to move them at all, let alone return them to the water. Unsupported by water, the weight of large whales tends to crush them internally and any attempts to move them often causes further damage. The most useful thing you can do is to report such a stranding to your local wildlife authority or police.

Small whales have a much greater chance of survival. Authorities still need to be informed as soon as possible of any stranding, but while you are waiting for them, there are basic first-aid procedures you can use to increase the chances of survival of individual animals.

There are new techniques for dealing with mass strandings. The surviving animals are taken from the stranding beach by truck or trailer and reunited in a quiet waterway nearby before being released as a group. This has proved very successful, as at Augusta in WA in 1986, when 96 out of 114 long-finned pilot whales were returned to the sea. These mass events are very complicated logistically, being coordinated by experienced people and requiring the help of many others; if you are prepared to help, your assistance will usually be appreciated but wear a wetsuit to keep warm.

Cetacean researchers often attend strandings, motivated by a desire to understand and care for the animals and perhaps learn something new about them and why they strand. Research may involve cutting open dead whales to see what they have been eating, or whether parasites, pollution or disease have affected them. This may be distressing for onlookers, as may the need for killing suffering animals that are beyond hope of rescue, so be prepared.

FIRST-AID PROCEDURES FOR STRANDED WHALES

- DO NOT try to return the animals to the sea without expert advice as you may injure them or separate them from family members, causing great distress.
- Roll the animal upright, without using its fins or flippers as levers. Beware of flukes and teeth, as the animal may be stressed and it could unwittingly injure you.
- Rinse sand away from the eyes and blowhole while they are closed.
- Orient the animals up the beach so their heads are pointed away from breaking waves.
- Keep the skin moist, either by regularly pouring water over the body or by covering the animal with wet sheets or blankets. Sunburn and dehydration are killers for cetaceans.
- Comfort the whale by speaking quietly or not at all, and stroking it gently. Stay where it can see you, and avoid sudden movements and loud sounds.
- Unless spectators are willing to help, ask them to stand back and talk quietly to avoid further stress to the whales. Large crowds should stay well back.
- If possible, identify the first animal ashore, as it may be the key to the stranding.

WHALE-WATCHING SITES

The most spectacular whale-watching locations can be well-populated tourist havens or remote townships with unusual names. They can be cliff tops, lighthouses, huge bays or fishing channels that weave their way between busy industrial ports. Since most people in Australia and New Zealand live near the coast, the only effort required to see a dolphin or whale is a short journey to the closest beach. Whales migrate past most of Australia's coastline on the east, west and south of the continent.

This part of the book lists the places where you can see whales or dolphins from land or sea. The Australian section is divided into States and, beginning at Queensland, it progresses clockwise around the coast to Western Australia. However, the Northern Territory is not included as the more commonly seen species in Australia's waters – such as the humpback whale and the southern right whale – do not migrate this far north. Also, while some dolphins, including the Indo-Pacific humpbacked dolphin, may be sighted off the shores of the Northern Territory and bottlenose and Irrawaddy dolphins are occasionally seen in Darwin Harbour, sightings are not regular and there are no specific land-based vantage points. The New Zealand section, also clockwise, starts from Paihia on the northern tip. Major sites have maps and general information about the whales that occur there, the location (including distances by road and highway numbers), types of accommodation available and what else is on offer when conditions do not favour whale sightings. The Resources section at the back of the book provides details of local tourist organisations to contact for more information.

Enough is known about the migration routes of the humpback and southern right whales to provide a guide as to what time of year they may be seen. The specific months listed under each site indicate when the boat trips operate or when whales are most often sighted. But remember that they may also be seen outside these "peak periods", so always keep an eye out for blows. Unfortunately, not enough is known about most other species (such as orcas, sperm and pilot whales) to indicate peak months. Bottlenose dolphins and common dolphins can be seen all year round in some areas.

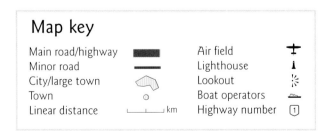

Map key

Main road/highway	▰	Air field	✈
Minor road	▬	Lighthouse	🗼
City/large town	◁	Lookout	⚲
Town	○	Boat operators	⚓
Linear distance	└─┴─┘ km	Highway number	①

QUEENSLAND

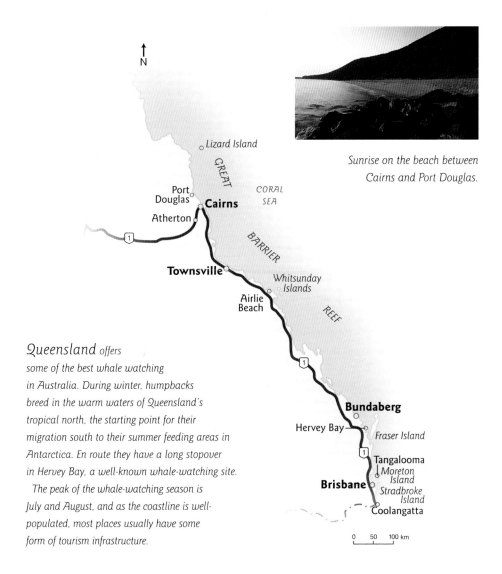

N

Lizard Island

GREAT

CORAL
SEA

Port
Douglas
Cairns

Atherton

1

BARRIER

Townsville

Whitsunday
Islands

Airlie
Beach

REEF

1

Bundaberg

Hervey Bay

Fraser Island

1

Tangalooma
Moreton
Island

Brisbane

Stradbroke
Island

Coolangatta

Sunrise on the beach between
Cairns and Port Douglas.

*Queensland offers
some of the best whale watching
in Australia. During winter, humpbacks
breed in the warm waters of Queensland's
tropical north, the starting point for their
migration south to their summer feeding areas in
Antarctica. En route they have a long stopover
in Hervey Bay, a well-known whale-watching site.
  The peak of the whale-watching season is
July and August, and as the coastline is well-
populated, most places usually have some
form of tourism infrastructure.*

0   50   100 km

CAIRNS, PORT DOUGLAS

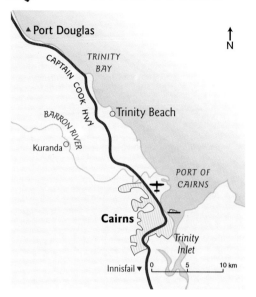

Species: Dwarf minke whales (March–October, peak June and July); Bryde's whales in the far northern reefs (off Lockhart River in Cape York country) may be sighted in December.

Location: Cairns is 1717 km north of Brisbane and 345 km north of Townsville via Bruce Hwy (1).

Accommodation: Hotels, motels, youth hostels, caravan parks and resorts; in the nearby Atherton Tablelands, farmstays and cottages. Lodge and resort accommodation is available on Green and Fitzroy islands.

Population: Cairns 68,000; Port Douglas 2100.

Other Attractions: Kuranda Scenic Railway and Skyrail, from Cairns; Royal Flying Doctor Service Visitors Centre; Esplanade Walking Trail to the Pier Marketplace; Great Barrier Reef cruises, Green and Fitzroy islands.

Over the past few years, scientists from the Museum of Tropical Queensland and James Cook University have been monitoring interactions between swimmers and dwarf minke whales on the Great Barrier Reef by observing and recording the actions of whales that voluntarily approach commercial dive boats. You can join the whales and snorkel along the Ribbon reefs that stretch from Cairns north to Lizard Island (boat trips depart from Princes Wharf, Pixie St, Port Douglas). Dwarf minkes are seen on the Great Barrier Reef between March and October, with most sightings during June and July in the northern reef waters. While this is a rare opportunity to interact with whales in their own environment, remember to adhere to the whale-watching guidelines, both for your own safety and that of the whales.

TOWNSVILLE

Only a few humpbacks migrate as far north as Townsville, so these whales are rarely seen there. Those humpbacks that do migrate this far north tend to pass on the seaward side of Magnetic Island and don't remain in the area for long, making it less likely that they will be seen from the mainland. However, Indo-Pacific humpbacked dolphins can be seen in the harbour, bottlenose dolphins farther out in the bay and, very rarely, Irrawaddy dolphins. Occasionally dolphins and whales are sighted from the ferry from Townsville to Magnetic Island, so it's always worth keeping an eye out, and the local radio station 4TO (HOT FM, 102.3) will broadcast any sightings that are reported.

WHITSUNDAY ISLANDS

Species: Humpback whales (July–September).

Location: Airlie Beach is 1275 km north of Brisbane via Bruce Hwy (1), and 26 km north-east of Proserpine.

Accommodation: Mainland: motels, budget-style, luxury resorts or self-contained villas; islands: resorts ranging from family-style to wilderness retreat, club and five-star, or charter a yacht or a houseboat.

Population: Airlie Beach 2700.

Other Attractions: The Great Barrier Reef; wildlife park; tandem skydiving; scenic seaplane and helicopter flights; parasailing; markets; rainforest tours; golf; fishing; arts and crafts; museums; sailing and other water sports.

The tropical climate of the Whitsunday Islands makes this area a very pleasant destination for whale watching, especially during the winter months. Humpbacks mate and calve in the waters along this part of the Queensland coast, so take care not to disturb breeding adults and mothers with calves. Boat trips to see humpbacks in the Whitsunday Islands depart from Shute Harbour or Abel Point Marina on Airlie Beach. About 85 per cent of the region is marine and mainland national park and many of the islands have high vantage points.

Aerial view of the Whitsunday Islands and Shute Harbour.

HERVEY BAY

Species: Humpbacks (July–October); bottlenose; very occasionally, Risso's dolphins.

Location: 300 km north of Brisbane via Bruce Hwy (1).

Accommodation: Good range of serviced apartments and motels; plenty of park and holiday accommodation.

Population: 31,000.

Other Attractions: Safe waters for swimming, catamarans and sailboards – there is no surf in Hervey Bay. Hiking, 4WD or guided tours on Fraser Island.

World Heritage-listed Fraser Island protects Platypus Bay, within the Hervey Bay Marine Park, from prevailing winds. As well as providing warm weather in winter and safe beaches, it provides a sheltered area for humpbacks resting on their southward migration. A well-established boat-based industry has developed in Hervey Bay, offering cruises from half a day to a full week. Because this is an area of intense tourism activity during the whale-watching season (which peaks in August), it is vital to respect the regulations citing the maximum number of boats with any pod of whales, minimum distances and appropriate behaviour around whales. Boat trips depart locally from Urangan and Pialba, and from Burnett Heads near Bundaberg, 372 km north of Brisbane. Sometimes researchers take out visitors; they use sailing vessels, which are less disturbing for whales than motor-powered boats. Bottlenose and humpbacked dolphins are also seen fairly regularly at Tin Can Bay just south of Hervey Bay. Dugongs also frequent the area.

Humpback whales perform at Hervey Bay.

TANGALOOMA, MORETON ISLAND

Species: Bottlenose dolphins; occasionally, humpback whales (July–November) and Indo-Pacific humpbacked dolphins.

Location: Moreton Island is accessible by vehicle ferry from Scarborough or Lytton.

Accommodation: Resort or camping (need to obtain a permit from national park rangers or ferry operators).

Population: 262 (Moreton Island).

Other Attractions: The island is mostly national park: hiking, swimming, sailing, fishing; coastal dunes, lakes, wetlands and forests.

Moreton Island consists entirely of sand and driving is only possible with 4WD vehicles. At Tangalooma, on the west coast of the island, bottlenose dolphins come in each night and there is a supervised feeding program at the resort (site of a former humpback whaling station). The Cape Moreton lighthouse is good for whale watching, as is the cliff-face just below it (researchers conducting population surveys of humpback whales often use this spot). You may also see Indo-Pacific humpbacked dolphins, which occur north of the Tweed River.

 # NORTH STRADBROKE ISLAND

Species: Humpbacks (June–November); very occasionally, pilot whales (although these are unlikely to come inshore).

Location: Fast water taxis or vehicle ferries operating from Cleveland in Brisbane to Dunwich on North Stradbroke Island.

Accommodation: One hotel, several caravan parks and holiday units plus camping on North Stradbroke Island.

Population: 800 (Point Lookout).

Other Attractions: Fishing; surfing; bushwalking along Blue Lake.

High cliffs at Point Lookout and Whale Rock Blowhole on North Stradbroke Island have a good reputation for whale watching. Boat trips depart from Scarborough on Moreton Bay (north-east of Brisbane's city centre).

NEW SOUTH WALES

New South Wales has fantastic whale-watching possibilities because the coastline is dotted with cliffs and headlands that provide excellent land-based lookouts. The best vantage points are the strategic locations of lighthouses.

Humpback whales regularly migrate along the coast. In northern NSW the best months for whale watching are in the middle of their migration (July–September) whereas in southern NSW it's possible to see them at the beginning (May–June) and end (November–December) of their migration. Humpbacks are the most commonly seen large whales, although sperm and pilot whales (the short-finned species and, occasionally, the long-finned species in cooler south coast waters) can also be seen further out at sea, especially along the edge of the continental shelf. Orcas and southern right, blue, false killer and Bryde's whales are also seen from time to time. Bottlenose dolphins can often be seen close to shore as well as off-shore, with common dolphins offshore. Less common species such as fin and minke whales also appear occasionally.

Tweed Heads
Byron Bay
Broken Head
Lennox Head
Evans Head
Iluka
Yamba
Coffs Harbour
Sawtell
Nambucca Heads
South West Rocks
Korogoro Point
Crescent Head
Point Plomer
Port Macquarie
North Haven
Diamond Head
Crowdy Head
Taree
Tuncurry
Forster
Seal Rocks
Port Stephens
Nelson Bay
Newcastle
Tweed River
Manning River
SOUTH PACIFIC OCEAN
Sydney
Stanwell Tops
Wollongong
Huskisson
Jervis Bay
Ulladulla
Batemans Bay
Dalmeny
Kianga
Narooma
Bermagui
Bega
Tathra
Merimbula
Eden
0 50 100 km
N

Fishing boats at Coffs Harbour jetty.

 TWEED HEADS

Species: Bottlenose, common and Indo-Pacific humpbacked dolphins.
Location: 862 km north of Sydney via Pacific Highway (1).
Accommodation: Small selection of motor inns; caravans and camp sites at nearby Tweed Heads South or Tweed Heads West.
Population: 10,200.
Other Attractions: Aboriginal cultural centre; laser-beam lighthouse on Point Danger headland.

Tweed Heads is quieter than Coolangatta, its sister city on the Queensland side of the border and it offers a more relaxed environ-ment for whale watchers. It's predominantly a fishing village but there's an extensive harbour leading into the Tweed River, with a number of charter boats offering trips to see dolphins. A good lookout base from land is Hastings Point, 20 km south.

 BYRON BAY

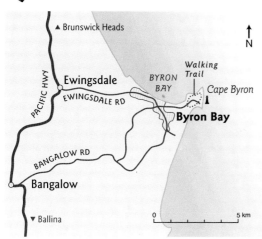

Species: Humpbacks (June–October); bottlenose dolphins; occasionally orcas.
Location: 830 km north of Sydney via Pacific Hwy (1).
Accommodation: Luxury resorts, beach houses and farmstays, and everything in between.
Population: 5000.
Other Attractions: Excellent beaches; surfing; hang-gliding; blues festival each April.

Byron Bay is one of the best sites in Australia to see humpbacks from land. As the most easterly point on the continent, the headland at Cape Byron provides an excellent platform to see whales as they round the "corner" of Australia. Numbers peak in the last week of June and the first week of July when they are migrating northwards, and during September–October when heading south. To get the best view, follow the scenic walking trail or drive up to Cape Byron lighthouse where the 100-metre-high cliffs provide a superb vantage point: researchers often take part in population counts here. Cape Byron is also famous for its surfing bottlenose dolphins. The cape has coin-operated telescopes. Diving is very popular in Byron Bay as tropical waters from the Coral Sea meet cooler southerly offshore currents, attracting unusual marine life.

The lighthouse and cliffs at Cape Byron are ideal for whale watching.

BROKEN HEAD, LENNOX HEAD, EVANS HEAD

South of Byron Bay, Broken Head Nature Reserve and Lennox Head are good spots to look for whales. Try Whites Head and Ballina Head, near Ballina, and Evans Head (32 km south of Ballina following the coast road), which has spectacular 180° views of the open ocean, making it a good vantage-point.

ILUKA

Iluka and Yamba (694 km north of Sydney), on either side of the Clarence River estuary, both feature fantastic beaches with white sand, azure water and few people. Around Iluka, there are many side roads through Bundjalung National Park, including one to Fraser Reef, where breaching humpbacks can be sighted. No car ferry exists between Iluka and Yamba, so it is a 40 km trip via the Pacific Hwy round to Yamba. The Clarence River estuary provides a fast-flowing area of water punctuated by islands, channels and inlets, and ideal feeding conditions for bottlenose dolphins. Any bridge is a good lookout point.

COFFS HARBOUR

Grafton ▲

↑ N

○ Moonee Beach

PACIFIC HWY

Split Solitary Island ○

SOLITARY ISLANDS MARINE RESERVE

Coffs Harbour

Muttonbird Island

▼ Nambucca Heads

0   5 km

Species: Humpbacks (June–October); bottlenose and common dolphins.
Location: 578 km north of Sydney via Pacific Hwy (1).
Accommodation: A range of resorts, motor lodges and motor inns plus a selection of holiday units, cabins and tourist parks.
Population: 22,000.
Other Attractions: Leisure parks featuring waterslides; flora reserves; walking tracks; zoo; fishing; pet-porpoise pool; diving and snorkelling in the marine reserve.

Muttonbird Island, off Coffs Harbour, is an excellent land-based site for spotting humpbacks. Stay on the marked tracks to avoid collapsing the burrows of muttonbirds (wedge-tailed shearwaters), which nest here from late August to May. At Coffs Harbour, the boat operators boast a six-month whale-watching season (June–December) but realistically most humpbacks have passed by the end of October. Coffs offers some of the most reasonably priced boat-based whale watching in NSW and, with its regular sightings and well set-up marina, it is fast becoming a popular alternative to the often crowded boats at Hervey Bay, in Queensland.

SAWTELL, NAMBUCCA HEADS, SOUTH WEST ROCKS

Sawtell (570 km north of Sydney) has a small boat-based whale-watching industry. Nambucca Heads has no whale-watching boats, but Lions Lookout on Ulrick Rd, and the Captain Cook Lookout and Rotary Lookout on Parkes St, offer good views across Shelly Beach and the heads. At 134 m above sea level, the lighthouse at Smoky Cape near South West Rocks is worth a visit. On several river ecotours leaving South West Rocks, dolphin sightings are a regular highlight and whale-watching trips will run if there are sufficient people.

KOROGORO POINT, CRESCENT HEAD, POINT PLOMER

Korogoro Point at Hat Head, a small settlement 459 km north of Sydney, provides a great vantage point for spotting migrating humpbacks with regular sightings from June to October. Crescent Head's Skyline Lookout, 13 km south, has potential for seeing whales, and Point Plomer has another good lookout, although it is a long detour off the main road. A 2.5 km circular walking track traverses Hat Head to Korogoro Point. Views are best from the high route along the ridge from the saddle, or take the lower path to the arch and cave.

PORT MACQUARIE

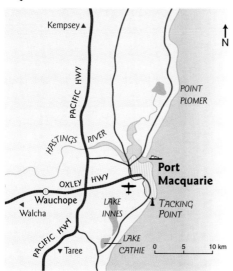

Species: Humpbacks (June–October); bottlenose dolphins.

Location: 407 km north of Sydney via Pacific Hwy (1).

Accommodation: Numerous multi-level resort buildings in town; more-secluded tourist villages, bed and breakfasts, beach units and caravan parks can be found further afield.

Population: 33,700.

Other Attractions: Wildlife park; nature reserve; observatory; rainforest centre; cruises; camel treks; canoeing.

Situated at the heart of the temperate Central Coast, Port Macquarie has a thriving pleasure-cruise industry that benefits from regular sightings of bottlenose dolphins in the Hastings River. It also has a small but dedicated boat-based whale-watching industry, although sometimes operators request a minimum number of people before they will go out looking for whales.

The Hastings River at Port Macquarie supports an active dolphin-watching industry.

NORTH HAVEN, DIAMOND HEAD, CROWDY HEAD, MANNING RIVER

On the southern outskirts of Port Macquarie is Tacking Point Lighthouse (5 km from the town centre). You can park at the lighthouse's base and take a walking track from here to other lookouts. A couple of boat operators are based at North Haven, and the Charles Hamey and Pilot Station lookouts at Perpendicular Point are good. National parks rangers report sightings of humpbacks from Diamond Head (about 11 km south of North Haven, not to be confused with Diamond Beach) and Crowdy Head another 42 km south, but plan your route as some roads are 4WD only. Although Taree is 4 km upstream from the mouth of the Manning River, dolphins have been sighted from the bridge, so keep an eye out as you cross. The Manning River was also home to a wandering Bryde's whale for several months in 1995.

FORSTER, TUNCURRY

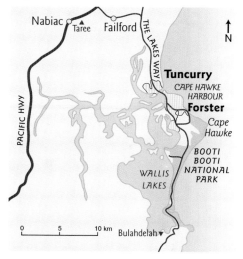

Species: Bottlenose (inshore); common dolphins (offshore); humpback whales (June–October).

Location: 312 km north of Sydney via Pacific Hwy (1).

Accommodation: Wide selection of motor inns and holiday apartments, plus plenty of camping and caravan parks.

Population: 18,000 (combined population of Forster and Tuncurry).

Other Attractions: Oyster festival (October long weekend); food and wine festival (September); annual triathlon (May); pleasure-boat hire; deep-sea fishing; dive charters; or hike through the narrow strip of low-lying land in Booti Booti National Park, bordered on one side by sheltered freshwater and on the other by open surf beaches.

The twin towns of Forster and Tuncurry are divided by the narrow entrance to Wallis Lakes, which creates a very turbulent flow of water through the Cape Hawke Harbour. Such waters are a good source of food for bottlenose dolphins, which are often sighted from the bridge. With bottlenose dolphins close to shore, common dolphins offshore and humpback whales in season, this region is a good bet for some form of whale watching, both land- and boat-based. One operator is licensed to take people swimming with common dolphins: one swimmer at a time dons snorkel and mask, climbs into the water and holds onto a rope strung alongside the boat to watch the playful dolphins. Inside the harbour, hire canoes and dinghies provide opportunities for individual dolphin encounters. There are several good land-based sites along the south side of the harbour.

SEAL ROCKS

Although fairly remote, Seal Rocks (38 km from Bulahdelah and 280 km north of Sydney) is a popular site for whale watchers and some loyal enthusiasts meet here regularly for breakfast. Particularly good early in the morning, the headland provides an elevated spot for seeing blows in winter. Seal Rocks was the site of a mass stranding of false killer whales in 1992.

PORT STEPHENS, NELSON BAY

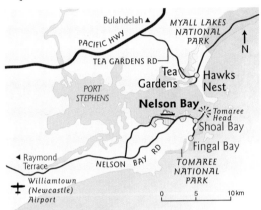

Species: Bottlenose dolphins; humpbacks (May–July, September–November).
Location: 245 km north of Sydney via Pacific Hwy (1), turn-off at Raymond Terrace.
Accommodation: Luxury waterfront apartments to cottages, bed and breakfasts and caravan parks.
Population: Nelson Bay 6700.
Other Attractions: Aquatic reserve for swimming, snorkelling and scuba diving; winery; toboggan park.

Port Stephens is a mecca for dolphin lovers. The various boat operators cater for all tastes and budgets, with inexpensive, safe boats for families through a range of speedier boats to glamorous yachts and catamarans. Some are designed to be taken out of the sheltered waters of the bay and into the ocean. Others carry a boom net for riding in the water alongside the craft, or boast a broad viewing platform at the bow of the boat that enables many people to watch dolphins bow-riding. A code of ethics among the operators prevents boats from chasing dolphins and limits the number of boats with a pod to no more than three. The aim is to avoid harming the estimated 100 resident bottlenose dolphins.

Most of the operators are based on the south side of Port Stephens at Nelson Bay, with a couple based at the northern side at the much quieter Tea Gardens. Even the ferry that makes the crossing between Nelson Bay and Tea Gardens advertises dolphin watching as a regular highlight. Tomaree Lookout just south of Nelson Bay provides a good vantage point from land for both dolphins in the harbour and whales in the open sea.

NEWCASTLE

The coastline around Newcastle (162 km north of Sydney) offers several good vantage points at nature reserves along the coast, in particular Redhead Bluff lookout and Redhead Point at Awabakal Nature Reserve just south of the city. Nine kilometres north of The Entrance, roughly halfway between Newcastle and Sydney, check out the lighthouse at Norah Head.

 SYDNEY

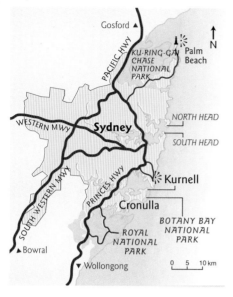

Species seen: Humpbacks (June–November); occasionally southern right whales (May–October), bottlenose and common dolphins.

Location: 870 km from Melbourne via the Hume Hwy/Freeway (31); 1100 km from Brisbane via the Pacific Hwy (1).

Accommodation: From high-rise luxury hotels or harbourside apartments to back-packer hostels, studio units and houseboats.

Population: 3.7 million.

Other Attractions: Cafes, museums, art galleries, theatre, surf and harbour beaches, harbour cruises, Sydney Opera House and Harbour Bridge, and national parks. Also great sporting and cultural events, including the Sydney Festival every January.

The noise pollution from busy shipping lanes in the ocean outside Sydney Harbour creates an obstacle course for humpbacks. The whales have, however, grown accustomed in part to this intrusion on their migratory path and can still be seen regularly from North and South

View from Barrenjoey Lighthouse at Palm Beach on Sydney's northern beaches.

SYDNEY WHALING

In the early to mid-1800s, Mosman Bay and Neutral Bay hummed with the hustle and bustle (and stench) associated with whaling stations, where the blubber of sperm and right whales was boiled down.
The only remnants are a few towers on old Mosman homes, originally used by whalers' families as lookouts.

heads as well as from other headlands along the surrounding coastline. To the south of Sydney, overlooking Botany Bay and the South Pacific Ocean, is Kurnell headland, a favoured spot among dedicated whale watchers. Enter through Botany Bay National Park (fee required). To the north, the lighthouse on Barrenjoey Head at Palm Beach makes a good whale-watching look-out. Bottlenose dolphins can on occasion be seen in Pittwater, Botany Bay, Sydney Harbour and some beaches.

🔭 WOLLONGONG

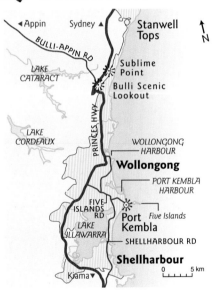

Species: Humpbacks (June–November); also, sperm, pilot, minke and beaked whales.
Location: 79 km south of Sydney via Princes Hwy (1).
Accommodation: Hotels; apartments; caravan parks and holiday accommodation in the surrounding region.
Population: 211,000.
Other Attractions: Hang-gliding from nearby Stanwell Tops; art and craft shops.

Port Kembla Harbour is the main destination for many ships and tankers, and this creates an obstacle course for passing humpbacks. On the drive south from Sydney to Wollongong, however, there are plenty of excellent elevated lookouts, so stop and pull out the binoculars for a look from Bulli Scenic Lookout (69 km south of Sydney) or Sublime Point Lookout (63 km south of Sydney), both easily spotted along the Princes Hwy. Also try Port Kembla Scenic Lookout on Military Rd, Port Kembla, offering panoramic views of Wollongong Harbour, Shellharbour to the south and, offshore, the Five Islands Bird Sanctuary and World War II fortifications.

The only boat-based whale-watching operator in Wollongong departs from Belmore Basin in Wollongong Harbour. It goes a long way out to sea in search of sperm and pilot whales, which tend to linger at the edge of the continental shelf looking for squid. Humpbacks are regularly sighted, but fin, minke and beaked whale sightings are a rarer delight. Owing to the distance, these trips are usually full days and are more suited to experienced sea-goers.

HUSKISSON, JERVIS BAY (ACT)

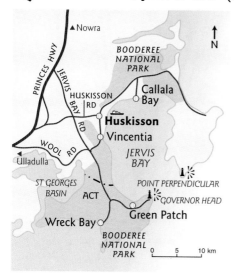

Species: Bottlenose dolphins; humpbacks (June–November); occasional orcas, pilot and sperm whales.

Location: 180 km south of Sydney via Princes Hwy (1).

Accommodation: Hotels, motels and apartments; lots of caravan and camping facilities in the area.

Population: Huskisson 3300.

Other Attractions: Good fishing; scuba diving; maritime museum; heritage complex.

Jervis Bay is renowned for its white sandy beaches and azure waters. From Huskisson, a large, multi-level boat regularly cruises with the bottlenose dolphins. This area is great for land-based whale watching because it has elevated cliffs and projects further onto the continental shelf than anywhere else on Australia's east coast, a geographical aspect that is thought to provide good food for toothed whales. If you have your own boat, head to Booderee National Park (entry fee required), previously called Jervis Bay National Park, and follow Green Patch Rd to the boat-launching ramp. For a good lookout, visit the remains of the old lighthouse near Governor Head. The northern side of the bay has another lighthouse at the spectacular Point Perpendicular, and the semi-resident pod of bottlenose dolphins is often sighted from the numerous beaches all along the bay.

Jervis Bay's tranquil waters are home to bottlenose dolphins.

ULLADULLA

No specific boat-based whale watching operates out of Ulladulla (231 km south of Sydney), but if you have a large enough group, one of the local dive operators will take you out. Warden Head just east of the town makes a good place to spot humpbacks from land, and as with all the towns along the south coast, you're more likely to see humpbacks on their southern migration (September–November).

BATEMANS BAY

Species: Bottlenose dolphins; humpbacks (June–November).

Location: 280 km south of Sydney via Princes Hwy (1); 150 km south-east of Canberra.

Accommodation: Good range of motor inns and apartments, plus caravan park and holiday accommodation.

Population: 9500.

Other Attractions: Great surfing beaches; good seafood; cruises on the Clyde River.

Just north of Batemans Bay, at a little beach off Long Beach in the bay, bottlenose dolphins are often seen cruising along the shoreline. Humpbacks swim further out from the coastline here, and the local boat operators often have to travel several kilometres out to sea before finding whales. These operators offer trips during the southern migration (September–November) and are based at the marinas along Clyde St. Any cliffs close to a coastline make good whale-watching spots, and humpbacks have been sighted frequently from Moruya Heads (turn east at Moruya, 28 km south of Batemans Bay).

Boats must go several kilometres offshore from the Clyde River at Batemans Bay to find whales.

 KIANGA, DALMENY

Two kilometres north of Narooma, take the turn-off to Kianga and Dalmeny, a scenic loop that returns to the Princes Hwy. There are some good places along the shoreline for spotting bottlenose dolphins. A Kianga boat operator often sees humpbacks during September–November.

 NAROOMA

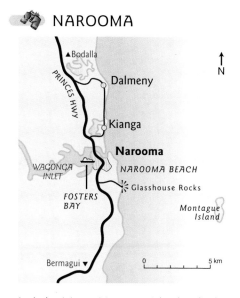

Species seen: Humpbacks (September–November).
Location: 349 km south of Sydney via Princes Hwy (1).
Accommodation: A range of motels and holiday units, plus caravan park and holiday accommodation ranging from farmstays to well-catered camping sites.
Population: 3400.
Other Attractions: Swimming; surfing; golf; diving; fishing; birdwatching; bushwalking; nearby Deua and Wadbilliga national parks.

Set at the mouth of the Wagonga Inlet, Narooma has several boat operators offering whale-watching trips and these can also include visits to Montague Island and other wildlife such as seals, little penguins, bottlenose and common dolphins or a combination. The tourist office provides a central point of reference, but a better option is to go directly to the jetty, which is down a steep hill just at the north end of the main shopping stretch. Most whale trips depart from here, so you can check out all the options by dealing directly with the captain. Other trips depart from the jetty at a marina in Fosters Bay in Wagonga Inlet. The best lookout from land is at Clifftop Park (not signposted: follow Glasshouse Rocks Rd in Narooma to the end of the dirt and past the cemetery), which offers views over Montague Island and Narooma Beach.

BERMAGUI, TATHRA

Along this stretch of the coast, it is worth taking a detour off the Princes Hwy and taking the more scenic coastal route, although it is not always possible to follow a sealed road all the way along the coast. Bermagui (350 km south of Sydney and 34 km south of Narooma) is more of a game-fishing village but charter operators will take whale watchers out if the group has sufficient numbers. Similarly, Tathra (440 km south of Sydney and 18 km east of Bega) has no real whale-watching industry, but humpbacks are seen passing very close to the cliffs fairly regularly. While both towns can be accessed by sealed roads leading off the Princes Hwy, the coastal road linking Bermagui and Tathra is mostly dirt.

MERIMBULA

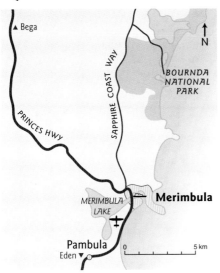

Species: Humpbacks (September–November); occasionally blue whales.

Location: 455 km south of Sydney via Princes Hwy (1).

Accommodation: Motels, serviced apartments, caravan parks, bed and breakfasts, holiday units and beach cabins.

Population: 4400.

Other Attractions: Family recreation park; Bournda National Park; vibrant fishing charter industry; beaches.

The incredible blue-green hues of Merimbula's water makes it a popular family holiday destination, particularly as the sandbar offers sheltered swimming beaches. The boat operators here work in cooperation with whale-watching boats at Eden to the south, communicating by radio to help locate humpbacks. Most whale-watching trips depart from the public jetty opposite the Lakeview Hotel and a variety of small fishing charter boats provide a good selection of whale-watching vessels. Scenic flights are also available (ask at Merimbula Airport or the tourist office).

EDEN, TWOFOLD BAY

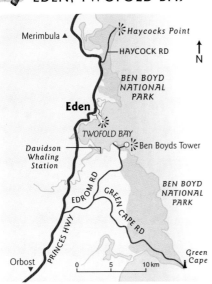

Species: Humpbacks (October–December); bottlenose dolphins in the bay; occasionally orcas, southern right (May–October), blue and minke whales.

Location: 476 km south of Sydney via Princes Hwy (1); 54 km south of Bega.

Accommodation: Motels, caravan parks and holiday units.

Population: 3100.

Other Attractions: Eden Killer Whale Museum (in Imlay St); Davidson Whaling Station (37 km south-east of Eden on the Kiah Inlet); Ben Boyd National Park and the chip-mill feature displays of the local logging industry; horse-riding; canoeing; game fishing.

When whales visit the deep waters of Twofold Bay, a siren sounds in Eden to alert whale-watchers.

Eden's beautiful deepwater harbour offers many opportunities for whale watching. The boat-based whale-watching industry here is unique in its cooperative approach: each of the operators offers a different type of charter and they all work together so that customers really benefit. Choose from a leisurely half-day cruise with dedicated whale people, an outing in a speedier boat that also has a good sightings record, or a fast trip in a small, powerful boat that goes out only if it has a confirmed whale sighting.

Eden is also one of the few places in Australia where humpbacks and, occasionally, blue whales can be seen feeding. Find out more at the Eden Killer Whale Museum, which organises the annual whale festival in October, and hosts a series of information evenings with visiting whale researchers. There's a fascinating link between Eden's history and a pod of remarkable orcas. In the early whaling days, the story goes, orcas would help the whalers round up and kill humpback and southern right whales. The reward for the orcas was the tongue and lips of the slaughtered whale – obviously a delicacy in their view!

The museum itself is a good lookout, as is Rotary Park at the ocean end of Imlay St. Eight kilometres north of Eden, turn off to Haycock Point, where southern right whales may be seen. To the south, follow the bay around to the Ben Boyd Lookout tower (18 km), built for whalers, or drive further south to the lighthouse at Green Cape (26 km from the highway turn-off, mostly dirt). Davidson Whaling Station is testament to Australia's whaling history with the whalers' cottage still standing and there are interpretative signs on the beach describing the "try-pots" used for boiling down blubber.

VICTORIA

Victoria's whale-watching industry is based mainly along the west coast where, in season, people can see the magnificent, broad backs of southern right whales. While there are some sightings of humpbacks in far eastern Victoria, many of the larger whale species don't occur along the central coast. However, a growing number of boat operators are offering swim-with dolphin programs, especially around the Port Phillip Bay area.

Sunset on the coast between Port Fairy and Yambuk.

 GABO ISLAND

Just south of the NSW border with Victoria, Gabo Island provides an opportunity to see humpbacks early in their migration north. They arrive from the Antarctic as early as May or June, and when they reach mainland Australia they tend to hug the coastline until they arrive at their summer destination somewhere in the Great Barrier Reef or Coral Sea. On their southward journey the last straggling humpbacks swim past Gabo Island as late as December, and have been seen breaching. The lighthouse on the island provides an excellent lookout, and the lighthouse keeper has a theory that the breaching is a signal or farewell before the whales strike out for the Antarctic. No commercial charters are available so access to the island is by private boat only, usually from Mallacoota.

POINT HICKS

Visitors to Point Hicks Lighthouse, in the heart of Croajingolong National Park, are fortunate to see humpbacks almost on their doorstep, sometimes as close as 50–100 m from shore. The whales head north from mid-May to mid-July then return in October–November (heading south). You can stay in one of two old cottages belonging to former lighthouse keepers where you can relax on the wide verandahs and look out to sea for blows, as well as seals and birds, or you can camp 3 km away at the Mueller and Thurra rivers. Access to Point Hicks and the lighthouse is by a 50 km dirt road (a 1-hour trip) from Cann River. For the more adventurous, take a canoe out on the nearby rivers or snorkel over the wreck of the ss *Saros*.

 ## LAKES ENTRANCE

Whether you're sailing, fishing, kayaking, windsurfing or even in a paddle boat, Lakes Entrance (319 km east of Melbourne) provides good opportunities for watching bottlenose dolphins in each of the Gippsland Lakes. They are often seen close to shore and around the entrances to lakes and waterways. Cruise-boat operators report regular sightings at the mouth of the Gippsland Lakes, which is only a couple of kilometres from Lakes Entrance.

 ## WILSONS PROMONTORY

While offering superb bushwalking and camping, as well as being home to large colonies of seals and birds, Wilsons Promontory offers few opportunities for whale watching. However, the local rangers do see the occasional humpback or southern right whale passing.

 ## SORRENTO, QUEENSCLIFF, PORT PHILLIP BAY

Species: Bottlenose dolphins, occasionally southern right whales (May–September); offshore, humpbacks (May–July, November); common dolphins.

Location: Sorrento is 100 km southeast of Melbourne via Nepean Hwy (3); Queenscliff is accessible from Sorrento via ferry, or by road from Melbourne via Geelong (103 km).

Accommodation: Caravan parks with cabins and camping grounds, as well as hostels, cottages and apartments.

Population: Queenscliff 2000; Sorrento 1200.

Other Attractions: Collins Settlement historic site; aquarium; bike paths.

Inside Port Phillip Bay it is possible to see the fins of meandering bottlenose dolphins at any time of the year, from many of the Melbourne suburbs and nearby towns that line the bay. South of the bay in the open sea are common dolphins, southern right whales and the occasional humpback. Sorrento is on the Mornington Peninsula on the far south-east side of the bay, and several boat operators based here offer trips where you can swim with dolphins or seals in summer (they usually provide wetsuits and snorkel gear). While seals make charming swimming companions, their smell will make your nose wrinkle! The boats also follow pods of bottlenose dolphins and people are placed at regular intervals on a line of rope attached to the aft of the boat. If you're in the water when the dolphins swim past, keep your snorkel on and your head down – you may catch only a fleeting glimpse but it will be worth it. But be warned – even in summer the water in Port Phillip Bay may only get to 19°C. Whales and dolphins have been spotted from Seaford (40 km south-east of Melbourne), Blairgowrie (100 km south-east of Melbourne) and Cape Schanck/Gunnamatta (92 km south-east of Melbourne). More dolphin and seal boat trips are available at Queenscliff on the Bellarine Peninsula, which has rolling surf on the ocean side and quiet beaches on the bay side suitable for swimming and boating.

 # WARRNAMBOOL

Species: Southern right whales (May–October); occasionally humpbacks (June–November); very occasionally, blue whales.
Location: 260 km south-west of Melbourne on the Princes Hwy (1).
Accommodation: Bed and breakfasts, motor inns, family apartments, hotels and numerous caravan parks.
Population: 25,500.
Other Attractions: Maritime museum; trout farm; cheese factory; markets; Tower Hill Game Reserve, an extinct volcanic crater now home to hundreds of birds.

Warrnambool (260 km south-west of Melbourne) is Victoria's top spot for seeing whales from land and is a known nursery ground for southern right whales. Every year a few whales calve or bring their calves close to shore at Logans Beach, and may remain in the area for several weeks. There is a viewing platform at the beach: follow the "whale" signs from the highway and cross the Hopkins River. Between May and October, you may see whales here, but do rug up – whale watching needs lots of patience and the winters here are cool! Boat charters are also available from the Breakwater Jetty in Warrnambool. If you are driving to Warrnambool from Melbourne, the Great Ocean Road along the Otway coast provides excellent whale-watching opportunities.

The whale lookout platform at Logans Beach, Warrnambool, offers reliable sightings during winter months.

PORT FAIRY, PORTLAND

Further west along the Victorian coast, Port Fairy was the base for the local whaling industry in the early 1800s. There is a lighthouse on nearby Griffiths Island, which is a good place to see whales. Portland, 362 km west of Melbourne, has lighthouses at Whalers Point (on Lighthouse St) and Cape Nelson, and a scenic lookout on Madeira Packet Rd. Whales are sometimes sighted from a regular seabird-watching charter boat.

TASMANIA

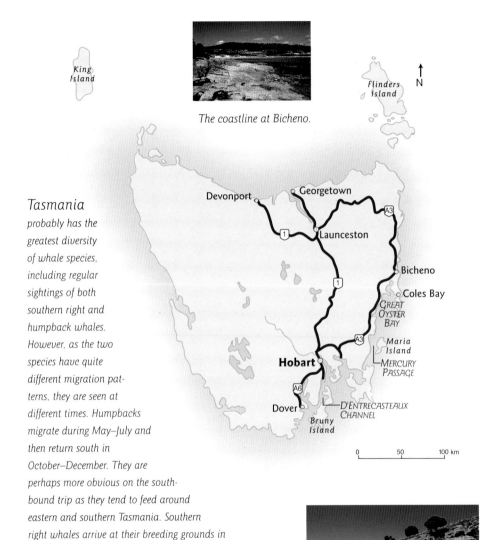

The coastline at Bicheno.

Tasmania probably has the greatest diversity of whale species, including regular sightings of both southern right and humpback whales. However, as the two species have quite different migration patterns, they are seen at different times. Humpbacks migrate during May–July and then return south in October–December. They are perhaps more obvious on the southbound trip as they tend to feed around eastern and southern Tasmania. Southern right whales arrive at their breeding grounds in Tasmanian waters in June and linger until October before migrating south again. Other species, although rarely seen, include orcas, sei whales, and dusky, common and southern right whale dolphins. Bottlenose dolphins are quite common in sheltered waterways along the east coast.

Painted Cliffs on Maria Island.

BICHENO

Sightings of humpbacks and southern right whales from land are sometimes reported at Bicheno and these whales can hang about for several days close to shore. The road from Bicheno south to Orford hugs the coastline and has lots of good vantage points for whale watching, especially the section along Great Oyster Bay. Bicheno is 182 km north-east of Hobart via the Tasman Hwy (A3). The area's other attractions include diving, fishing, wineries, a wildlife park and an aquarium.

COLES BAY

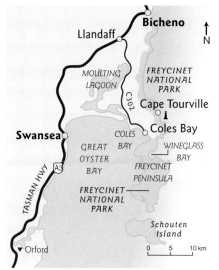

Species: Humpbacks (June–July, October–November); southern right whales (June–October); bottlenose dolphins.
Location: 206 km north of Hobart via Tasman Hwy (A3).
Accommodation: Small selection of cottages and lodges, backpacker hostels and camp sites (also in Freycinet National Park).
Population: 220.
Other Attractions: Walks to spectacular Wineglass Bay; birds at Moulting Lagoon.

Coles Bay on the Freycinet Peninsula is a small inlet within Great Oyster Bay. One boat offers whale-watching charters to seek southern right whales throughout winter and spring, humpback whales in spring and autumn, and resident bottlenose dolphins. Humpbacks sometimes feed here on their southward migration, and southern right whales occasionally calve in the bays. National park rangers can provide maps and advice on any number of scenic walks that offer whale-watching opportunities. These include a marked track to the summit of Mt Amos, or you can drive along the Sleepy Bay road to the lighthouse at Cape Tourville.

MARIA ISLAND

A national park, Maria Island is separated from mainland Tasmania by Mercury Passage. Migrating southern right whales sometimes come through this passage before entering Great Oyster Bay. Humpbacks may feed in the passage but most migrate along the seaward side of the island. Both species, as well as bottlenose dolphins, may be encountered during the ferry trip from Orford. There are no cars, electricity or shops on the island, so take all your own supplies if you wish to base yourself at one of the two camp sites and take your time exploring the fossil caves, historic settlement, ruins and painted cliffs.

HOBART

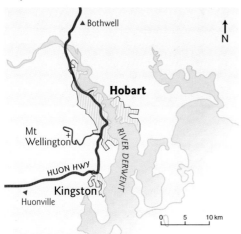

Species: Southern right whales (May–June); humpbacks (October–November); bottlenose and common dolphins.
Location: From Melbourne, either fly direct to Hobart or cross Bass Strait by car-ferry service and drive to Hobart, 249 km via Hwy A8 and Hwy 1.
Accommodation: Good selection of basic to stylish accommodation, including townhouses, hotels, motor lodges and backpacker hostels.
Population: 131,000.
Other Attractions: Drive or walk up Mt Wellington; the Australian Antarctic Division (at Kingston, 12 km south of Hobart) has information on whales; browse the historic buildings at Salamanca Place; go on a harbour cruise; experience the blizzard simulator at the Antarctic Adventure Centre (also at Salamanca Place).

Southern right whales are occasionally sighted between May and October in the sheltered waters of the River Derwent which, until the whaling years, was a calving ground. Humpbacks have been seen feeding at the mouth of the Derwent, and bottlenose and common dolphins are regularly sighted in coastal areas, where they come to feed.

BRUNY ISLAND

Species: Southern right whales (June–October) and humpbacks (May–July, October–December); occasional sightings of orcas, bottlenose and common dolphins.
Location: 35 km south of Hobart to Kettering on the Channel Hwy (B68) and then by ferry (1 hour).
Accommodation: Reasonable selection of places to stay, mostly cottages.
Population: 520.
Other Attractions: Lighthouse; Bligh Museum; Captain Cook's landing place; convict-built church; penguin-viewing platform; camel treks.

View over D'Entrecasteaux Channel from the neck of Isthmus Bay, Bruny Island.

Southern right whales are sometimes observed at Adventure Bay, south of the narrow strip of land in the middle of the island (June–October). Whale sightings and movements vary greatly from year to year: you may not see any whales at all, on the other hand you may be fortunate enough to see a newborn calf. The Cape Bruny lighthouse is a good viewing spot. Orcas have been seen herding common dolphins in Adventure Bay.

D'ENTRECASTEAUX CHANNEL

D'Entrecasteaux Channel has many vantage points along the shoreline where you may sight southern right whales, orcas, common dolphins or the resident bottlenose dolphins. The waterways here have many shallow bays and mudflats, which can be a trap for whales and dolphins. Dover, 82 km south of Hobart on the Huon Hwy (A6), is one of several towns in the region that offers cruises of the channel and the Huon River.

SOUTH AUSTRALIA

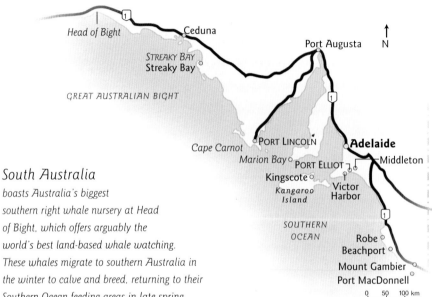

South Australia

boasts Australia's biggest
southern right whale nursery at Head
of Bight, which offers arguably the
world's best land-based whale watching.
These whales migrate to southern Australia in
the winter to calve and breed, returning to their
Southern Ocean feeding areas in late spring.
Southern right whales may be sighted anywhere
along the SA coast from May to October, peaking
in late July and August. Humpbacks rarely move
through these southern waters, heading instead
for warmer waters along Australia's east and
west coasts. Other whales occasionally seen in SA
waters include orcas, blue, fin, sperm, Bryde's,
minke, pilot and false killer whales. Bottlenose
dolphins are frequently seen close to shore, and
both common and bottlenose dolphins occur
further offshore.

*Scotts Cove viewed from Harveys Return
lookout on Kangaroo Island.*

PORT MACDONNELL, ROBE

There are several good vantage points for whale watching along the east coast of SA, including the quiet fishing village of Port MacDonnell (467 km south-east of Adelaide), the former whaling town of Beachport (385 km south-east of Adelaide) and Robe (339 km south-east of Adelaide). Each of these has limited accommodation; if you are after more choice, base yourself at Mount Gambier, close to the Victorian border.

PORT ELLIOT, MIDDLETON, GOOLWA

Three towns within easy reach of Adelaide are Port Elliot (91 km south), Middleton (88 km south) and Goolwa (83 km south). Each has numerous great lookouts for spotting southern right whales cruising the shoreline. At Port Elliot, try Freemans Nob at the end of the Strand. Between here and Middleton stop at Fishery Bay (Caravan Park Rd) and Bashams Beach (Seaview Rd). At Middleton, visit Middleton Point (off Mindacowie Ave); the Middleton Store Whale Information Centre; Chapman Rd car park (off Goolwa Rd); Surfers Parade (off Boetcher Rd); and the top of Surfers Parade (corner of Miami Boulevard). At Goolwa, stop in at the car park at the end of Beach Rd or ask about scenic flights at Goolwa Airport. As the range of accommodation is limited, an alternative is to base yourself at nearby Victor Harbor.

VICTOR HARBOR, ENCOUNTER BAY

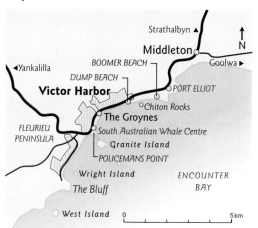

Species: Southern right whales (May–October).
Location: 85 km south-east of Adelaide, on the Fleurieu Peninsula.
Accommodation: Bed and breakfasts and guesthouses through to resorts and everything in between – hotels, motels and caravan parks.
Population: 10,000.
Other Attractions: Little penguin colony on Granite Island; wildlife park; fishing; diving; sailing; surfing; adventure park and miniature village; tourist railway; festivals; galleries.

Victor Harbor is a reliable land-based site for viewing southern right whales. A major attraction is the South Australian Whale Centre, featuring three floors of displays, exhibits, giant murals and information on Australia's whaling history and the marine environment. It also operates a Whale Information Service – phone ahead to see if any whales are in the area; whale sightings are reported on a separate number (see Resources section). This stretch of the Encounter Coast gets heavy pedestrian traffic, so keep to the paths to minimise erosion.

Respect private property and take care at all times – clifftops can be dangerous places. Good whale-watching spots are at both Bluff car parks (end of Franklin Pde); Policemans Point (end of Flinders Pde); The Groynes (Bridge Tce); Hayward St car park (off Hindmarsh Rd); Dump Beach (end of First Ave); Chiton Rocks (end of Fifth Ave); and Boomer Beach (end of Carfax St).

 ## KANGAROO ISLAND

Southern right whales (May–October), bottlenose and, rarely, dusky dolphins have been sighted from Kangaroo Island, particularly the south-east coast, including Pennington Bay and D'Estrees Bay, but also in Vivonne Bay and Weirs Cove. Travelling to Kangaroo Island on the regular vehicular ferry service from Cape Jervis across Backstairs Passage you might see southern right whales. The alternative is to fly and hire a car on the island. The biggest of the nine settlements is Kingscote (population 1400), where the ferry docks.

 # ADELAIDE

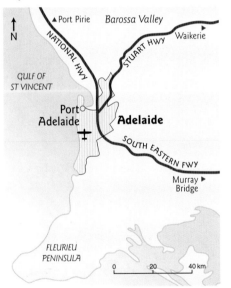

Species: Bottlenose dolphins.

Location: 1415 km from Sydney via Hume (3) and Sturt (20) hwys; 725 km from Melbourne via Western (8) and Dukes (1) hwys.

Accommodation: Ranges from basic hotels to multi-storey luxury complexes; caravan parks near the city centre.

Population: Over 1 million.

Other Attractions: Beautiful, historic buildings. Visit the nearby Barossa Valley for wine-tasting. The Adelaide Festival and Adelaide Fringe Festival are held in even-numbered years.

Adelaide has a small whale-watching industry with boat operators based on the coast in the northern suburb of Port Adelaide. Occasionally, bottlenose dolphins are seen from the city's beaches and they are regularly sighted in the Port River estuary. The South Australian Museum in North Terrace actively supports whale conservation and has a collection of whale and dolphin specimens, information, photographs and sightings. Flight packages are available, departing from Adelaide to Head of Bight, to see southern right whales.

 ## YORKE PENINSULA

Marion Bay on the very tip of the Yorke Peninsula provides a good vantage point for whale watching and is listed as one of SA's main whale-watching sites by the Department of Environment, Heritage and Aboriginal Affairs (DEHAA). A tiny fishing settlement (population

70), this holiday destination bordering Innes National Park is 370 km west of Adelaide. A small selection of park and holiday accommodation, such as units or cottages is available, with more variety at the bigger towns of Yorketown, Minlaton, Maitland or Kadina on the peninsula.

PORT LINCOLN, EYRE PENINSULA

Coach and 4WD trips depart from Port Lincoln (672 km west of Adelaide) to see southern right whales at Head of Bight. Locally, there are good lookouts from Sleaford Bay (covered in wildflowers from late winter to early spring) and Fishery Bay. Whalers Way, 32 km south of Port Lincoln, is the southernmost tip of the Eyre Peninsula and features a very dramatic, beautiful coastline, including cliffs, caves, crevasses, blowholes and beaches. You can camp at the Cape Carnot lookout; keys and camping permits are available at the tourist centre and most stores, motels and service stations. To explore Port Lincoln's history and see how it was settled by whalers, take a self-drive tour through the remains of the old whaling station along the privately owned Whalers Way, which also requires a permit.

STREAKY BAY

Common and bottlenose dolphins are often seen in and around Streaky Bay, 713 km west of Adelaide. While in the area, visit Point Labatt (55 km south), which has a permanent colony of Australian sea lions, a rare presence on the Australian mainland.

CEDUNA

Few southern right whales are sighted from Ceduna (783 km west of Adelaide), but 4WD safari tours connect with Adelaide flights and depart here to see southern right whales at Head of Bight (May–October). Camping permits for Head of Bight can be obtained here.

HEAD OF BIGHT

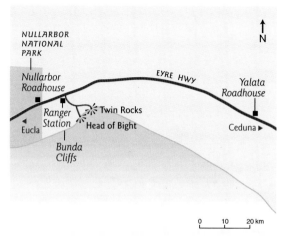

Species: Southern right whales (May–October); bottlenose dolphins.

Location: 1100 km from Adelaide.

Accommodation: Hotel/motel and caravan park at Nullarbor Roadhouse; units, caravan and camping at Yalata Roadhouse.

Population: Nullarbor Roadhouse, approximately 13 (staff); Yalata Roadhouse, about 100.

Other Attractions: Scenic flights from Nullarbor Roadhouse over the coast and inland to Maralinga.

The Head of Bight is arguably one of the world's best land-based whale-watching locations.

This is Australia's foremost southern right whale breeding area, with up to 100 whales in the area in peak season (August–September). Forty or more calves may be born here then, and mothers and calves remain until the calves are strong enough to migrate south. It is possible to get excellent views of calves as they exercise and socialise with their mothers and other whales, and of adults courting and mating, all within 100 m of the Bunda Cliffs. The whales are also frequently seen in the broad sandy bay near Twin Rocks. Many cetacean researchers base themselves at Head of Bight during the breeding season to collect data and make observations. Bottlenose dolphins and sea lions often accompany the whales, and great white sharks sometimes attack the calves. Humpback whales are sighted, but very rarely. Penguins, ospreys, wedge-tailed eagles, pink cockatoos, dingoes, hairy-nosed wombats and camels are all found in this area.

Head of Bight is managed jointly by Yalata Aboriginal Community and the SA Department of Land Management. Entry permits are required (available from the Yalata Roadhouse or the White Wells Ranger Station on the access road to the viewing area). A separate permit is required if you choose to camp in the Nullarbor National Park (available from the DEHAA; the closest one is in Ceduna). On clear still nights here you can sometimes hear the whales. The road and car parks are sealed, and there are boardwalks, viewing platforms and toilets. The Eyre Highway is an experience in itself and there are several points along the clifftops all the way to the WA border (185 km) that provide perfect vantage points for close-up viewing and photography, but plan the journey carefully – there are no fuel stops past the Nullarbor Roadhouse and you should take water and supplies.

A special package is available on the Trans-Australia Railway's Indian Pacific – travel as far as Cook by rail and then by coach to Head of Bight. Package tours are also available from Adelaide, Ceduna and Port Lincoln.

WESTERN AUSTRALIA

Western Australia's southern shores are visited by southern right whales between May and October. In June and July, humpback whales head north, returning southwards in September and November. As July is the wettest month in south-west WA, the southern migration times are better for watching whales. In between these times, the humpbacks are in their breeding area to the State's north-west.

Bottlenose dolphins are common in WA, with Monkey Mia being a well-known natural habitat for dolphin encounters. The WA Department of Conservation and Land Management (CALM) strictly monitors human–dolphin interaction to ensure dolphins are not harmed, so please support their efforts and heed their advice. To avoid dependency on humans, CALM now urges people not to feed dolphins.

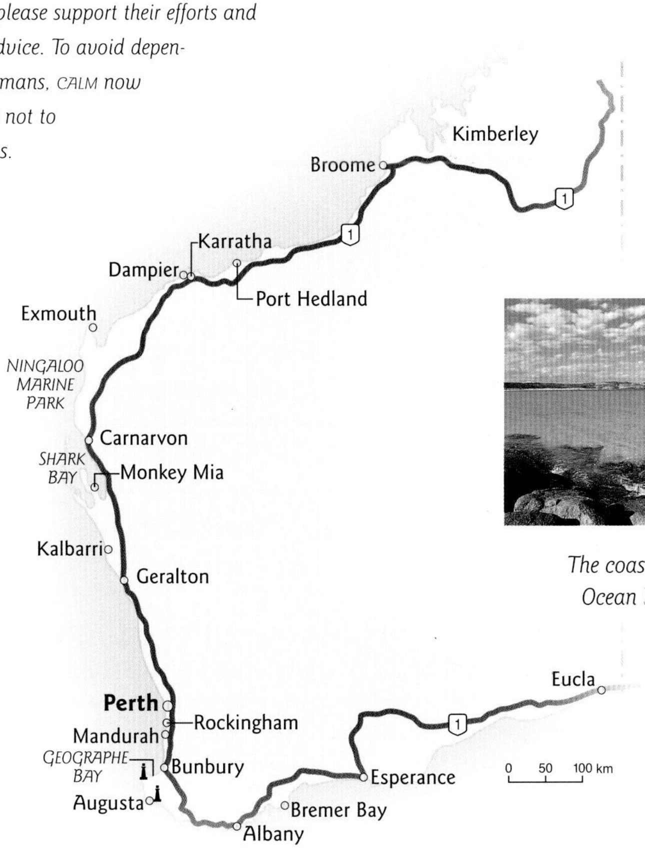

N

Kimberley

Broome

Karratha

Dampier

Port Hedland

Exmouth

NINGALOO MARINE PARK

Carnarvon

SHARK BAY

Monkey Mia

Kalbarri

Geralton

The coastline along Great Ocean Drive, Esperance.

Eucla

Perth

Rockingham

Mandurah

GEOGRAPHE BAY

Bunbury

Esperance

Augusta

Bremer Bay

Albany

0   50   100 km

EUCLA

In the south and east of the State, whale watching revolves around the movements of southern right whales in winter and spring. Good vantage points are the sandhills near Eucla, which is close to the SA border. It is also only about 200 km from Head of Bight, the favourite breeding and calving ground for the southern right whale.

 ESPERANCE

While there is no boat-based whale watching near Esperance (721 km east of Perth), there are several excellent land-based lookouts in the area. Travelling from Eucla, there are more at Twilight Cove and the Eyre Bird Observatory (both difficult 4WD access) near the town of Cocklebiddy; the area east of Israelite Bay; Cape Le Grand National Park; and Cape Arid National Park (120 km east of Esperance), an area that features sandplains, heathlands, beaches and granite headlands.

 **BREMER BAY**

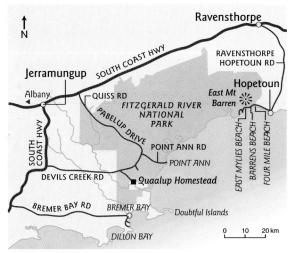

Species: Southern right whales (May–October); occasionally humpbacks.
Location: 515 km south-east of Perth via Albany Hwy (30) and South Coast Hwy (1).
Accommodation: Bremer Bay has one hotel/motel, two caravan parks, homesteads, a youth camp, bed and breakfast.
Population: 250.
Other Attractions: Boating; fishing; water-skiing; scuba diving; 4WDing; Wellstead Homestead museum.

Although a small town, Bremer Bay is situated in a region offering good whale-watching options. Cruises run from the town and there are vantage points along the coastline, including Point Ann in Fitzgerald River National Park. Here, in a mountain range stretching from Bremer Bay east to Hopetoun, is a UNESCO-designated biosphere containing some of the State's richest biological diversity. The area is accessible to 2WD and 4WD vehicles, with basic, limited overnight camping (bring all supplies, including water); toilets and gas barbecues at some beaches. You can stay at the Quaalup Homestead, which has cabins, meals, basic food supplies and barbecues (caravans are not allowed in the national park except for direct access to the homestead).

Southern right whales have been seen from East Mt Barren lookout, Four Mile Beach, Barrens Beach and East Mylies Beach but any lookout or headland in this region is suitable as the whales frequent the area from Point Ann south to Doubtful Islands, Bremer Bay and Dillon Bay.

ALBANY

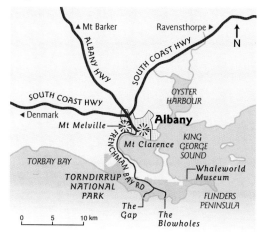

Species: Southern right whales (May–October); humpbacks (June–November).

Location: 408 km south of Perth via Albany Hwy (30).

Accommodation: Hotels, motels, guesthouses, cottages, chalets, flats and caravan and camping parks.

Population: 25,000.

Other Attractions: Surfing, bush-walking, wineries, wildflowers.

Albany has a historical connection to whales: the last animal killed by whalers in Australia was a sperm whale processed here in 1978. Today, Albany Whaleworld is an important reminder of the whaling industry and has a whalechaser vessel, spotter aircraft and whale skeletons.

Albany is on an impressive stretch of coast facing the Southern Ocean, straddled between Mt Clarence and Mt Melville, both of which provide spectacular views of migrating southern right whales and humpbacks. Following the coast around the harbour, visitors can look for whales while exploring The Gap (a 24 m drop to the sea) in Torndirrup National Park, the Natural Bridge, a huge piece of granite eroded to form an arch, and the Blowholes.

AUGUSTA

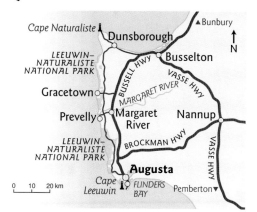

Species: Humpbacks (June–November); southern right whales (May–October); bottlenose dolphins; occasionally blue whales.

Location: 320 km south of Perth via South Western Hwy (1) and Bussell Hwy (10).

Accommodation: Hotel, motel, cottages, chalets and cabins.

Population: 460.

Other Attractions: This area features many caves, some open to the public.

Near Canal Rocks in Leeuwin-Naturaliste National Park, north of Augusta.

Whale-watching boats depart Augusta from June to September in search of southern right whales and humpbacks. In September, the operators move north and boats depart from Dunsborough to view humpbacks as they often stop to rest around Cape Naturaliste on their southward migration (September–November). Occasionally, blue whales and New Zealand fur seals are seen. Whale-watching flights and boat charters covering the sheltered waters of Flinders Bay are available from May to November. Visit the Cape Leeuwin Lighthouse, 8 km south of Augusta on Leeuwin Rd, where you will get a magnificent view of both the Southern and Indian oceans. A memorial and plaque on Davies Rd in Flinders Bay commemorates the successful rescue of 97 stranded false killer whales there in 1986.

Cape Naturaliste

Humpbacks migrate past Cape Leeuwin and Cape Naturaliste in late August and are often seen resting in Geographe Bay (September–December). The lighthouse at Cape Naturaliste (13 km north-west of Dunsborough) is a good observation spot, as are several of the walking trails. There is also a whale lookout. Explore Meelup Beach, Eagle Bay and Bunker Bay fronting Geographe Bay, and on the western side of the cape, the impressive formation called Sugarloaf Rock. A plaque at Castle Rock near Meelup Beach marks an old whaling station. Between Cape Naturaliste and Cape Leeuwin there are also many caves worth exploring.

 BUNBURY

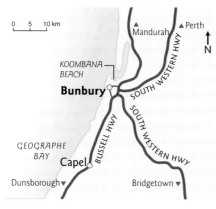

Species: Bottlenose dolphins; occasionally, southern right whales (May–October); humpbacks (June–July).

Location: 180 km south of Perth via Bussell Hwy (10).

Accommodation: Selection of hotel/motels, parks and holiday accommodation.

Population: 22,000.

Other Attractions: Migratory birds at the Capel wetlands and Bunbury's big swamp; tall timber country at Pemberton; wineries at Willyabrup and Margaret River.

At the Bunbury Dolphin Discovery Centre you can wade, swim or snorkel with bottlenose dolphins that come and go from Koombana Beach. There is an admission fee to the centre but playing with the dolphins is free. Although touching or feeding them is forbidden, CALM does allow some monitored feeding. The dolphins seem to prefer mornings visits but sometimes come twice a day. The centre includes audio-visual displays, exhibits and a viewing deck. Cruises in Geographe Bay and to nearby Dunsborough are also available.

MANDURAH

Bottlenose dolphins are seen frequently in the estuary at Mandurah (74 km south of Perth) and a couple of boats offer cruises within the Mandurah waterways and Murray River. The estuary is an important spawning area for larval fish, providing food for the dolphins.

ROCKINGHAM

Species: Humpbacks (June–July; September–November); bottlenose dolphins; occasionally southern right whales (May–October).

Location: 47 km south of Perth via Kwinana Freeway.

Accommodation: Some hotels and motels, but more choice in caravan park and holiday accommodation.

Population: 50,000.

Other Attractions: The area has sheltered waters and ocean beaches, good for swimming, surfing, snorkelling, sailing, fishing and crabbing.

You can swim with bottlenose dolphins at Rockingham; swimming tours depart daily from Val Street Jetty (October–June, wetsuits and snorkelling gear provided). There are sightseeing tours to Penguin Island and Seal Island where you can see little penguins, sea lions and rare birds. A ferry service operates between the islands and the mainland daily from September to June. Penguin Island closes during the penguins' breeding season from June to August.

 PERTH

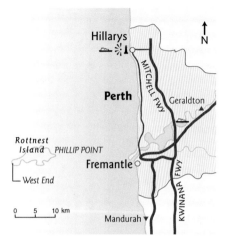

Species: Humpbacks (June–July; September–November); occasionally southern right whales (May–October).
Location: 2695 km from Adelaide; 4147 km from Darwin.
Accommodation: In the city, something for all tastes and budgets; holiday and caravan park accommodation in the suburbs.
Population: 1.2 million.
Other Attractions: Swan River cruises; wine-tasting in Swan Valley; miniature village; Perth Zoo; Northbridge cafes and restaurants; tram rides; botanic gardens; Yanchep National Park (50 km north).

Whale watching in the Perth region is based on the humpbacks migrating north from June to July and south from September to November. On their southward migration, newly pregnant females usually lead the way, followed by the sub-adult whales, mature males and females. Mothers with new calves come last, as they rest frequently and travel more slowly.

Charter boats operate through September–November from ferry terminals at Fremantle (19 km south of Perth) and Hillarys Boat Harbour (20 km north of Perth). Catch a coach from Perth to either terminal. Boat trips to Rottnest Island also leave from these terminals. Humpbacks, and occasionally blue whales, are often seen from the boardwalk at the west end of the island, or from the Bathurst lighthouse and Oliver Hill lookout at the east end. Here you can also snorkel or scuba dive with Australian sea lions.

The boardwalk at West End on Rottnest Island.

Dwarf minke whales have been sighted recently and may visit regularly in May to July. Rottnest Island is also inhabited by the quokka, a tiny, unusual wallaby.

The dolphin sanctuary at Underwater World at Hillarys Boat Harbour has daily feedings and on weekends you can snorkel and swim with the captive bottlenose dolphins.

KALBARRI

Species: Humpbacks (June–July; August–October).
Location: 589 km north of Perth, a 65 km detour off the North West Coastal Hwy (1).
Accommodation: Two hotel/motels, caravan park and holiday cabins.
Population: 820.
Other Attractions: Rainbow Jungle; wildflower centre; Kalbarri National Park.

Kalbarri has a boat- and land-based whalewatching industry. Choose one of the charter boats offering trips to see humpbacks or try the whale-watching tower at Rainbow Jungle (4 km south, admission charge) or hire a canoe to explore the Murchison River.

MONKEY MIA

Species: Bottlenose dolphins; humpbacks in Shark Bay (June–November).
Location: 750 km north of Perth via Brand and Coastal hwys (1), and 26 km north-east of Denham on the Peron Peninsula.
Accommodation: Choice of resort, lodge. cottage, villa and carvan park in Monkey Mia and Denham (26 km south-west).
Population: 300.
Other Attractions: Shark Bay Marine Reserve, which has dugongs, sea turtles and sharks; Shell Beach, a 60 km long beach compacted 10 m deep with shells.

Monkey Mia is world-renowned for the visiting bottlenose dolphins that regularly interact with humans. You can wade into knee-deep water and let the bottlenose dolphins approach you, or join in a regular feeding program, which is strictly monitored by CALM. CALM also runs the Dolphin Information Centre (admission charge). Just a reminder: these are wild animals, so encounters, although regular, can never be guaranteed. In July 1993, several Bryde's whales were filmed close to shore in Shark Bay feeding on densely packed anchovy schools.

 CARNARVON

There is a chance of sighting humpbacks (June–November) from the new jetty in Carnarvon (902 km north of Perth) or join a whale-watching boat trip. Learn about Australia's whaling history at the new Whale Museum on Babbage Island, or travel north along the North West Coastal Highway for 25 km before turning off for the sea cave blowholes and Point Quobba, where, from June to November, you may see passing humpbacks. Head another 230 km north and a couple more whale-watching boats leave from the main beach at Coral Bay, an area also renowned for manta rays, whale sharks and turtles.

 EXMOUTH

In some ways, Exmouth Gulf seems to mirror Hervey Bay on Australia's east coast, as it, too, offers a sheltered bay for humpbacks with new calves to rest on their southward migration during winter and spring. With a small boat-based whale-watching industry, Exmouth (1270 km north of Perth) also offers superb fishing, the chance to swim with whale sharks (a shark, not a whale, March–June), or snorkelling in the coral gardens on Ningaloo Reef.

The lighthouse on Vlamingh Head (19 km north of Exmouth) has coin-operated binoculars offering sweeping views of North West Cape, Ningaloo Reef and migrating whales.

The lagoon within Ningaloo Reef is also visited regularly by bottlenose dolphins. Small groups of Indo-Pacific humpbacked dolphins also occur within the reef from Tantabiddi Creek southwards. Occasionally they interact with the bottlenose dolphins.

 DAMPIER, KARRATHA

Dampier and Karratha (1535 km north of Perth) both have a small boat-based whale-watching industry focusing on humpbacks, but you can sometimes also see Indo-Pacific humpbacked dolphins. After touring some of the 42 islands in the Dampier Archipelago, you could explore the Pilbara gorges in Karijini National Park or Millstream–Chichester National Park.

 PORT HEDLAND

At 1762 km north of Perth via North West Coastal Hwy (1) or 1660 km via Great Northern Hwy (95) and 2678 km from Darwin, Port Hedland (population 16,000) offers a fledgling boat-based humpback whale-watching industry. Other attractions include flatback turtles, which nest in the area (September–Apil), and harbour cruises. A 26 m high observation tower behind the tourist bureau and overlooking the ocean is a great whale-watching spot (flat shoes are required for safety; not sandals or open shoes).

 BROOME

Species: Humpbacks (July–September); occasionally, Bryde's and minke whales; bottlenose, Indo-Pacific humpbacked, Irrawaddy and spinner dolphins; also dugongs.

Location: 2300 km north of Perth and 1900 km south-west of Darwin via Great Northern Hwy (1).

Accommodation: Hotels/motels, self-contained units, bed and breakfasts, caravan parks and backpacker hostels.

Population: 11,000.

Other Attractions: Famous Cable Beach – 22 km of white sand and clear water; Chinatown; wilderness safaris to the Kimberley; crocodile park; dinosaur footprints.

Humpbacks that migrate along the west coast have calving areas in the waters off the north-west of Australia that extend from Broome right to the top of the Kimberley. They have been seen from Broome, the Buccaneer Archipelago, and south of Adele Island, with peak sightings between August and September. Boat tours are available.

The azure waters of Gantheaume Bay, Broome, are often frequented by researchers studying humpbacks.

NEW ZEALAND

New Zealand is a popular destination for adventurous travellers, and
travel agents offer a comprehensive
range of fly-drive packages from
Australia. Most of the whale-watching industry in NZ focuses on boat-
based sightings and swimming opportunities with dolphins and other marine
mammals such as seals. Land-based
opportunities are fewer, although there
are cliff tops at Kaikoura where you
can see dusky dolphins and the
occasional sperm whale. Various
headlands along the north-east
coast of the North Island give a
commanding view where you
might be lucky.

Bay of Islands near the northern
end of North Island.

PAIHIA, NORTHLAND

Species: Bottlenose and common dolphins.

Location: 241 km north of Auckland and 898 km north of Wellington.

Accommodation: Motels, hotels, resorts and lodges.

Population: 2000.

Other Attractions: Cruises; fishing; diving; sailing; shipwrecks; Waitangi National Reserve.

Boat and swimming tours to see common and bottlenose dolphins are available all year round from Paihia in the Bay of Islands (71 km north of Whangarei), Mangonui in Doubtless Bay (154 km north of Whangarei), Tutukaka (27 km east of Whangarei) and Ruakaka in Bream Bay (28 km south of Whangarei). Orcas, false killer whales and Bryde's whales can also be spotted from dolphin trips at certain times of the year.

COROMANDEL PENINSULA

At Whitianga (199 km east of Auckland), you can swim with common dolphins all year round and with bottlenose dolphins in late winter and spring. Sometimes you can also see orcas. You can also swim with dolphins at Whangamata (165 km south-east of Auckland).

BAY OF PLENTY

Boats trips to see a variety of marine mammals depart from Tauranga (205 km south of Auckland and 546 km north of Wellington). There are swim programs at Whakatane (298 km south of Auckland and 545 km north of Wellington). These focus mostly on common dolphins but you can sometimes see bottlenose dolphins.

NAPIER

Marineland at Napier on the south-east coast of the North Island (357 km south of Auckland and 323 km north of Wellington) allows swimming with captive common dolphins. You can also see California sea lions, New Zealand fur seals, otters and penguins.

DISAPPEARING ACT

Although whaling in New Zealand stopped in 1962, the stream of migrating whales that once passed its shores has not returned. Possibly the whales may be migrating further off-shore, or this population may have been eradicated by whalers.

NELSON/MARLBOROUGH SOUNDS

In this area you can take part in a variety of activities involving marine mammals, from kayaking with seals to watching common or bottlenose dolphins. The activities based in Nelson (424 km from Christchurch) and Picton (336 km from Christchurch or three hours by ferry from Wellington), focus on boat-based dolphin watching, rather than swimming. In summer, you may also see Hector's dolphins, orcas, dusky dolphins and New Zealand fur seals.

KAIKOURA

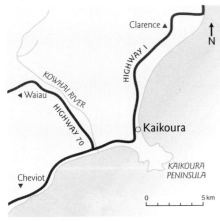

Species: Sperm whales; dusky and common dolphins; occasionally, Hector's dolphins, orcas and pilot whales.
Location: 183 km north of Christchurch.
Accommodation: Hotels, motels, guesthouses, hostels, farmstays, bed and breakfasts and camping grounds.
Population: 2000.
Other Attractions: Surfing; fishing; sailing; canoeing; white-water rafting; scuba diving; coastal walks; horse treks; traditional Maori art; limestone caves; Fyffe House (showing the history of whaling at Kaikoura).

Nestled in the shadow of the 2600 m high Kaikoura Range, Kaikoura is the only place in NZ with a predictable number of whales that specifically offers whale-watching tours – other whale-watching tour operators in NZ incorporate dolphins, seals and whales in their programs. The Kaikoura Peninsula is the meeting place for two strong ocean currents that converge in deep-water canyons. These canyons plunge to incredible depths just a few kilometres from the shore, resulting in a marine ecosystem rich in nutrients, creating an ideal feeding ground for sperm whales. You can choose from a boat tour to see the sperm whales or a swim program with dusky dolphins, common dolphins and seals all year round; scenic

Kaikoura township and the seaward Kaikoura Range.

flights are also available. There have been occasional sightings of other species such as southern right whale dolphins, pilot whales, bottlenose dolphins and orcas passing through the nearby Hikurangi Trench or "Whale Road", a deep ocean trench fairly close to shore.

 BANKS PENINSULA

Species: Hector's dolphin (all year round).
Location: 80 km south-east of Christchurch.
Accommodation: Akaroa has lots of holiday homes; Christchurch has motels, luxury hotels and apartments.
Population: Akaroa permanent population 700; around 3500 during tourist season.
Other Attractions: In Akaroa, nature harbour cruises; fishing; kayaking; horse trekking; scenic mail run; cheese factory.

Hector's dolphins are unique to New Zealand and are found most commonly and consistently in the waters around the Banks Peninsula. There is a choice of operators offering swim programs, with boats based at Akaroa. Penguins, seals and birdlife may also be seen.

PORPOISE BAY

Porpoise Bay is in the Bay of Te Waewae on the south-western side of the South Island. Boat trips depart to watch, but not swim with, Hector's dolphins. Te Waewae village is 76 km from Invercargill, the nearest main town. Hector's dolphins can also be seen at Curio Bay on Stewart Island, accessed by plane or ferry.

MILFORD SOUND

Bottlenose dolphins, seals and penguins can be seen from cruise ship or kayak in the Mirror Lakes and the Fiordland National Park, which are tucked away in the remote south-west of New Zealand. Te Anau has a small selection of motels, motor inns and lodges, or you can base yourself in Queenstown (307 km to the east).

GREYMOUTH

On the north-west coast of the South Island, boat trips to see Hector's dolphins are available in the Greymouth and Hokitika areas (258 km west of Christchurch). Swimming with dolphins is not allowed here but you can swim with the seals. Greymouth is the terminus for the TranzAlpine train that links the east and west coasts.

RESOURCES

TOURIST ORGANISATIONS

To obtain whale-watching information, start by consulting local tourist offices, listed here alphabetically for each State under the locations found in the guide to sites. Contact details, including, where available, email addresses and web sites (listed with the www. prefix) have been given. Whale information centres and State conservation departments and museums are also listed, where relevant, in the next section. Check with these sources, as well for up-to-date information as the whale-watching industry is constantly growing.

QUEENSLAND

Queensland Government Travel Centre
243 Edwards St
Brisbane 4001
Tel: (07) 3874 2800
Fax: (07) 3221 5320
Email: qgtc-brisbane@
qttc.com.au
www.queensland-travel-centre.com.au

Bundaberg
• Bundaberg District Tourist and Development Board
271 Bourbong St
Bundaberg 4670
Tel: (07) 4152 2333
Fax: (07) 4153 1444
Email: bundytour@
interworx.com.au
www.funzine.net/
bundaberg

Cairns
• Tourism Tropical North Queensland
51 The Esplanade
Cairns 4870
Tel: (07) 4051 3588

Fax: (07) 4051 0127
Email: ttnq@tnq.org.au
www.tng.org.au

Hervey Bay
• Fraser Coast South Burnett Regional Tourism Board
388–396 Kent St
Maryborough 4650
Tel: (07) 4122 3444
Fax: (07) 4122 3426
Email: info@frasercoast.org
www.frasercoast.org\

• Hervey Bay Central Booking Office
341 The Esplanade
Scarness 4655
Tel: (07) 4124 1300
or 1800 130 024
Fax: (07) 4128 1039
www.cbo.webjump.com.au

Moreton Island
• Redlands Tourism
152 Shore St West
Cleveland 4163
Tel: (07) 3821 0057
Fax: (07) 3821 3875
Email: redlandstourism@
redland.net.au

www.redland.net.au/
redlandstourism

North Stradbroke Island
• Stradbroke Visitors Centre
Junner St
Dunwich 4183
Tel: (07) 3409 9555
Fax: (07) 3409 9789
Email: redlandstourism@
redland.net.au
www.redland.net.au/
redlandstourism

Port Douglas
• Port Douglas Tourist Information Centre
23 Macrossan St
Port Douglas 4871
Tel: (07) 4099 5599
or 1800 809 999
Fax: (07) 4099 5070

Townsville
• Townsville Information Centre
The Strand
Townsville 4810
Tel: (07) 4771 3061
or 1800 801 902
Fax: (07) 4771 4361

Email: tel@tel.com.au
www.tel.com.au

Whitsunday Islands

• Whitsunday Information Centre
Bruce Hwy
Proserpine 4800
Tel: (07) 4945 3711
or 1800 801 252
Fax: (07) 4945 3182
Email: info@whitsunday
information.com.au

NEW SOUTH WALES

NSW Tourist Information

• The Sydney Visitors Centre
106 George St
Sydney 2000
Tel: 13 20 77
www.tourism.nsw.gov.au

Ballina

• Ballina Visitor
Information Centre
cnr River St & Las Balsas Plaza
Ballina 2478
Tel: (02) 6686 3484
Fax: (02) 6686 0136
Email: balinfo@balshire.org.au

Batemans Bay

• Batemans Bay
Visitor Centre
Princes Hwy
Batemans Bay 2536
Tel: (02) 4472 6900
or 1800 802 528
Fax: (02) 4472 8822
Email: eurovcb@acr.net.au
www.acr.net.au/eta/

Bermagui

• Bermagui Arts & Crafts Tourism
8 Lamont St

Bermagui 2546
Tel: (02) 6493 3054
• BP Service Station
8 Coluga St
Bermagui 2546
Tel/Fax: (02) 6493 4174

Broken Head: *see* Byron Bay

Byron Bay

• Byron Shire Visitors
Information Centre
80 Johnson St
Byron Bay 2481
Tel: (02) 6685 8050
Fax: (02) 6685 8533

Coffs Harbour

• Coffs Harbour Visitor
Information Centre
cnr Marcia St & Rose Ave
Coffs Harbour 2450
Tel: (02) 6652 1522
or 1800 025 650
Fax: (02) 6652 5674
Email: tourism@
coffscoast.com.au

Crescent Head

• Kempsey Visitor
Information Centre
Pacific Hwy
South Kempsey 2440
Tel: (02) 6563 1555
or 1800 64 2480
Fax: (02) 6563 1537
Email: ktic@midcoast.com.au
www.slnsw.gov.au/kempsey

Dalmeny: *see* Narooma

Eden

• Eden Visitors Centre
Imlay St
Eden 2551
Tel/Fax: (02) 6496 1953

• Davidson Whaling Station:
see Eden Visitors Centre

Evans Head

• Tourism Promotions
Richmond River Shire Council
PO Box 378
Casino 2470
Tel: (02) 6662 2066
Fax: (02) 6662 1342
Email: rrstour@nor.com.au
www.richmondnet.com.au/rrsc
• Silver Sands Caravan Park
Park St
Evans Head
Tel/Fax: (02) 6682 4212

Forster/Tuncurry

• Forster Visitor
Centre
Little St
Forster 2428
Tel: (02) 6554 8799
or 1800 802 692
Fax: (02) 6555 6185
Email: tourglc@tpgi.com.au
www.greatlakes.org.au

Huskisson/Jervis Bay

• Shoalhaven Visitor Centre
254 Princes Hwy
Bomaderry 2541
Tel: (02) 4421 0778
or 1800 024 261
Fax: (02) 4423 2950
Email: tourism@
shoalhaven.nsw.gov.au
www.shoalhaven.nsw.gov.au

Iluka

• Clarence River Tourist Assoc.
cnr Spring St & Pacific Hwy
South Grafton 2460
Tel: (02) 6642 4677

Fax: (02) 6643 1927
Email: crta@nor.com.au
Kianga: *see* Narooma
Korogoro Point: *see*
Cresent Head
Lennox Head: *see* Ballina
Merimbula
•Merimbula Tourist
 Information Centre
 Beach St
 Merimbula 2548
 Tel: (02) 6495 1129
 or 1800 670 080
 Fax: (02) 6495 4264
 Email: maccat@acr.net.au
 www.merimbula-tourism.
 com.au
Nambucca Heads
•Nambucca Valley Visitor
 Information Centre
 Pacific Hwy
 Nambucca Heads 2448
 Tel: (02) 6568 6954
 or 1800 646 587
 Fax: (02) 6568 5004
Narooma
•Narooma Visitor Centre
 Princes Hwy
 Narooma 2546
 Tel: (02) 4476 2881
 Fax: (02) 4476 1690
 Email: eurovcn@acr.net.au
 www.acr.net.au/eta
Nelson Bay: *see* Port Stephens
Newcastle
•Newcastle Tourism
 92 Scott St
 Newcastle 2300
 Tel: (02) 4974 2999
 Fax: (02) 4929 6732

Email: newtour@
hunterlink.net.au
www.ncc.nsw.gov.au
North Haven
•Kew Visitor Information
 Centre
 Pacific Hwy
 Kew 2439
 Tel: (02) 6559 4400
 or 1800 803 447
 Fax: (02) 6559 4709
Port Macquarie
•Port Macquarie Visitor
 Information Centre
 cnr Clarence & Hay Sts
 Port Macquarie 2444
 Tel: (02) 6581 8000
 or 1800 025 935
 Fax: (02) 6581 8010
 Email: vicpm@
 midcoast.com.au
 www.portmacquarie
 info.com.au
Port Stephens
•Port Stephens Visitor
 Information Centre
 Victoria Pde
 Nelson Bay 2315
 Tel: (02) 4981 1579
 or 1800 808 900
 Fax: (02) 4984 1855
 Email: tops@hunterlink.
 net.au
 www.portstephens.org.au
Sawtell: *see* Coffs Harbour
Seal Rocks: *see* Forster
South West Rocks: *see*
Crescent Head
Sydney: *see* NSW Tourist
Information

Taree
•Manning Valley Visitor
 Information Centre
 Old Pacific Hwy
 Taree North 2430
 Tel: (02) 6552 1900
 Fax: (02) 6552 3889
 Email: manningvic@
 gtcc.nsw.gov.au
 www.gtcc.nsw.gov.au/tourism
Tathra
•Tathra Wharf Trading Post
 & Information Centre
 Wharf Rd
 Tathra 2550
 Tel: (02) 6494 4062
Tea Gardens
•Tea Gardens Visitor
 Information Centre
 Myall St
 Tea Gardens 2324
 Tel: (02) 4997 0111
Tuncurry: *see* Forster
Tweed Heads
•Tweed Heads Visitor
 Information Centre
 4 Wharf St
 Tweed Heads 2485
 Tel: (07) 5536 4244
 or 1800 674 414
 Fax: (07) 5536 4204
 Email: info@tactic.
 nsw.gov.au
 www.tactic.nsw.gov.au
Ulladulla
•Ulladulla Visitor Centre
 Civic Centre
 Princes Hwy
 Ulladulla 2539
 Tel: (02) 4455 1269

Fax: (02) 4454 0889
www.shoalhaven.nsw.gov.au/
Wollongong
• Tourism Wollongong
93 Crown St
Wollongong 2500
Tel: (02) 4227 5545
Fax: (02) 4228 0344
www.wollongong.nsw.
gov.au/weblink/

VICTORIA

Victoria Visitor Information
Centre
cnr Swanston & Little Collins Sts
Melbourne 3000
Tel: (03) 9658 9955
or 13 28 42
Fax: (03) 9650 6168
www.tourism.vic.gov.au
Lakes Entrance
• Lakes Entrance Visitors Centre
cnr Marine Pde &
The Esplanade
Lakes Entrance 3909
Tel: (03) 5155 1966
or 1800 637 060
Fax: (03) 5155 1324
Point Hicks
• Point Hicks Lighthouse
Point Hicks Rd
via Cann River 3890
Tel/Fax: (03) 5158 4268
Port Fairy
• Port Fairy & Region Visitor
Information Centre
22 Bank St
Port Fairy 3284
Tel: (03) 5568 2682
Fax: (03) 5568 2833

Portland
• Portland Maritime
Discovery Centre
Lee Breakwater Rd
Portland 3305
Tel: (03) 5523 2671
or 1800 035 567
Fax: (03) 5521 7287
Queenscliff: *see* Sorrento
Sorrento
• Sorrento Visitor
Information Centre
2 St Aubins Way
Sorrento 3943
Tel: (03) 5984 5678
Fax: (03) 5984 4044
Warrnambool
• Warrnambool Visitor
Information Centre
600 Raglan Pde
Warrnambool 3280
Tel: (03) 5564 7837
or 1800 637 725
Fax: (03) 5561 2133

TASMANIA

Tourism Tasmania
110 Collins St
Hobart 7000
Tel: (03) 6230 8250
or 1800 806 846
Fax: (03) 6230 8232
Email: tasinfo@
tourism.tas.gov.au
www.tourism.tas.gov.au

SOUTH AUSTRALIA

South Australia Travel Centre
1 King William St
Adelaide 5000

Tel: (08) 8303 2222
Fax: (08) 8303 2249
www.visit-southaustralia.
com.au
Adelaide: *see* South
Australia Travel Centre
Ceduna
• Ceduna Gateway Visitor
Information Centre
58 Poynton St
Ceduna 5690
Tel: (08) 8625 2780
or 1800 639 413
Fax: (08) 8625 3294
Email: travelce@tpg.com.au
Goolwa: *see* Victor Harbor
Head of Bight
• Nullarbor Hotel Motel
PMB 30
Ceduna 5690
Tel: (08) 8625 6271
Fax: (08) 8625 6261
• Yalata Roadhouse
c/o CMA Yalata
via Ceduna 5690
Tel: (08) 8625 6986
Fax: (08) 8625 6987
Email: yalata@bigpond.com.au
www.yalatawhales.vicnet.
gov.au
Kangaroo Island
• Kangaroo Island Gateway
Visitor Information Centre
Howard Drive
Penneshaw 5222
Tel: (08) 8553 1185
Fax: (08) 8553 1255
Email: tourki@kin.on.net
www.tourkangarooisland.
com.au

Middleton

• Middleton Store
  Main Rd
  Middleton 5213
  Fax: (08) 8554 2064
  see also: Victor Harbor

Mount Gambier

• Lady Nelson Visitor &
  Discovery Centre
  Jubilee Hwy East
  Mount Gambier 5290
  Tel: (08) 8724 9750
  or 1800 087 187
  Fax: (08) 8723 2833
  Email: theladynelson@mount
  gambiertourism.com.au
  www.mountgambier
  tourism.com.au

Port Elliot: *see* Victor
Harbor

**Port Lincoln/Eyre
Peninsula**

• Port Lincoln Visitor
  Information Centre
  66 Tasman Tce
  Port Lincoln 5606
  Tel/Fax: (08) 8683 3544
  or 1800 62 9911
  Email: plvic@camtech.net.au

Port MacDonnell, Robe:
see Mount Gambier

Streaky Bay

• Shell Roadhouse
  & Tourist Centre
  Alfred Tce
  Streaky Bay 5680
  Tel/Fax: (08) 8626 1126

Victor Harbor

• Victor Harbor Tourist
  Information Centre

The Causeway
Victor Harbor 5211
Tel: (08) 8552 5738
Fax: (08) 8552 5476

• South Australian Whale Centre
  2 Railway Tce
  Victor Harbor 5211
  Tel: (08) 8552 5644
  Fax: (08) 8552 5142
  Email: whale@webmedia.
  com.au
  www.webmedia.com.au/whales/

• Whale Information
  Service/hotline
  Tel: 1900 931 223
  To report whale sightings
  Tel: (08) 8552 5644

Yorke Peninsula

• Moonta Visitor
  Information Centre
  Blanche Tce
  Moonta 5558
  Tel: (08) 8825 1891
  Fax: (08) 8825 2930

WESTERN AUSTRALIA

WA Tourist Centre
  Albert Facey House
  cnr Wellington St &
  Forrest Place
  Perth 6000
  Tel: (08) 9483 1111
  or 1300 361 351
  Fax: (08) 9481 0190
  Email: travel@tourism.
  wa.gov.au
  www.tourism.wa.gov.au

Albany

• Albany Tourist Bureau
  Old Railway Station

Proudlove Pde
Albany 6330
Tel: (08) 9841 1088
or 1800 644 088
Fax: (08) 9842 1490
Email: albanytb@
ominnet.net.au
www.wobbleweb.com.
au/albany

• Whaleworld
  Frenchman Bay Rd
  Albany 6330
  Tel: (08) 9844 4021
  Fax: (08) 9844 4621
  Email: whalewld@
  albanyis.com.au

Augusta

• Augusta Tourist
  Information Centre
  70 Blackwood Ave
  Augusta 6290
  Tel: (08) 9758 1695
  Fax: (08) 9758 0107

Bremer Bay

• Bremer Bay Tourist
  Information Centre
  5 Gnombup Tce
  Bremer Bay 6338
  Tel: (08) 9837 4093
  Fax: (08) 9837 4180

• Dept of Conservation &
  Land Management
  120 Albany Hwy
  Albany 6330
  Tel: (08) 9842 4500
  Fax: (08) 9841 7105
  www.calm.wa.gov.au

Broome

• Broome Tourist Bureau
  cnr Broome & Bagot Rds

Broome 6725
Tel: (08) 9192 2222
Fax: (08) 9192 2063
Email: tourism@broom.
wt.com.au
www.ebroome.com/tourism

Bunbury

• Bunbury Visitor
  Information Centre
  Old Railway Station
  Carmody Place
  Bunbury 6230
  Tel: (08) 9721 7922
  or 1300 656 202
  Fax: (08) 9721 9224
  Email: welcome@
  bunburytourism.org.au
  www.bunburytourism.org.au
• Dolphin Discovery Centre
  Koombana Drive
  Bunbury 6230
  Tel: (08) 9791 3088
  Fax: (08) 9791 3420
  Email: dolphin2@dolphin
  discoverycentre.asn
  www.livingwindows.
  gateway.net.au

Cape Naturaliste

• Cape Naturaliste Tourism
  Association
  38 Peel Tce
  Busselton 6280
  Tel: (08) 9752 1288
  Fax: (08) 9754 1470
  Email: bsntb@
  highway1.com.au
  www.capeweb.com.
  au/escape
• Dunsborough Tourist Centre
  Seymour Boulevard

Dunsborough 6281
Tel: (08) 9755 3299
Fax: (08) 9756 8065
www.capeweb.com.
au/escape

Carnarvon

• Carnarvon Tourist Bureau
  Civic Centre
  Carnarvon 6701
  Tel: (08) 9941 1146
  Fax: (08) 9941 1149

Coral Bay

• Coral Bay Tourist Association
  Coral Bay Arcade
  Robinson St
  Coral Bay 6701
  Tel/Fax: (08) 9942 5988
  Email: coralbayturtle@
  bigpond.com.au

Dampier: *see* Karratha

Esperance

• Esperance Tourist Bureau
  Museum Village
  Dempster St
  Esperance 6450
  Tel: (08) 9071 2330
  Fax: (08) 9071 4543
  Email: visit.esperance@
  bigpond.com.au

Eucla

• Eucla Motor Hotel
  Eyre Hwy
  Eucla 6443
  Tel: (08) 9039 3468
  Fax: (08) 9039 3401

Exmouth

• Exmouth Tourist Bureau
  Murat Rd
  Exmouth 6707
  Tel: (08) 9949 1176

Fax: (08) 9949 1441
Email: exmouth-tour@
nwc.net.au
www.exmouth-australia.com

Kalbarri

• Kalbarri Tourist Bureau
  Grey St
  Kalbarri 6536
  Tel: (08) 9937 1104
  or 1800 639 468
  Fax: (08) 9937 1474

Karratha

• Karratha Tourist Bureau
  Karratha Rd
  Karratha 6714
  Tel: (08) 9144 4600
  Fax: (08) 9144 4620

Lancelin

• Lancelin Accommodation &
  Tourist Information
  102 Gingin Rd
  Lancelin 6044
  Tel/Fax: (08) 9655 1100

Mandurah

• Mandurah Tourist Bureau
  75 Mandurah Tce
  Mandurah 6210
  Tel: (08) 9550 3999
  Fax: (08) 9550 3990
  Email: pdc@mandurah.
  wa.gov.au

Monkey Mia

• Dolphin Information Centre
  Shark Bay
  Monkey Mia 6537
  Tel: (08) 9948 1366
  Fax: (08) 9948 1512
• Shark Bay Tourist Bureau
  71 Knight Tce
  Denham 6537

Tel: (08) 9948 1253
Fax: (08) 9948 1065

Perth: *see also* WA Tourist
Centre

• Fremantle Tourist Bureau
Town Hall, Kings Square
High St
Fremantle 6160
Tel: (08) 9431 7878
Fax: (08) 9431 7755
Email: holzwart@
wantree.com.au
www.holidaywa.net.au

• Underwater World
West Coast Highway
Hillarys Boat Harbour 6025
Tel: (08) 9447 7500
Fax: (08) 9447 7856
Email: uwperth@
wantree.com.au
www.coralworld.com

• Rottnest Island Visitor Centre
Main Jetty
Rottnest Island 6161
Tel: (08) 9372 9752
Fax: (08) 9372 9755
www.rottnest.wa.gov.au

Port Hedland

• Port Hedland Tourist Bureau
13 Wedge St
Port Hedland 6721
Tel: (08) 9173 1711
Fax: (08) 9173 2632

Rockingham

• Rockingham Tourist Centre
43 Kent St
Rockingham 6168
Tel: (08) 9592 3464
Fax: (08) 9592 2778
Email: rtc@iinet.net

NEW ZEALAND

New Zealand Visitor Centre
America Cup Village
Viaduct Quay
cnr Hobson & Quay Sts
Auckland
Tel: (09) 979 7005
Email: nzvc@aucklandnz.com

Akaroa

• Akaroa Information Centre
80 Rue Lavaud
Akaroa
Tel/Fax: (03) 304 8600

Banks Peninsula:
see Akaroa

• Christchurch-Canterbury
Visitor Centre
cnr Worcester St & Oxford Tce
Christchurch
Tel: (03) 379 9629
www.christchurch
tourism.co.nz

Bay of Islands: *see* Paihia

Bay of Plenty

• Tauranga Visitor &
Travel Centre
80 Dive Crescent
Tauranga
Tel: (07) 578 8103

Coromandel Peninsula

• Coromandel Information
Centre
355 Kapanga Rd
Tel: (07) 866 8598

Greymouth

• Greymouth Information
Centre
cnr Herbert & Mackay Sts
Greymouth
Tel: (03) 768 5101

Kaikoura

• Westend
Kaikoura
Tel: (03) 319 5641

Milford Sound: *see* Te Anau

Napier

• Napier Visitor Centre
100 Marine Pde
Napier
Tel: (06) 834 1911

• Marineland
Marine Pde
Napier
Tel: (06) 834 4027
www.marineland.co.nz

**Nelson, Marlborough
Sounds**

• Nelson Visitor Centre
cnr Trafalgar & Halifax Sts
Tel: (03) 548 2304
Fax: (03) 546 9008

Paihia, Northland

• Bay of Islands Information
Centre
Marsden Rd
Paihia 0252
Tel: (09) 402 7345
Fax: (09) 402 7314
Email: paivin@nzhost.co.nz

Picton

• Picton Visitor Information
Centre
Foreshore, Picton
Tel: (03) 573 7477

Porpoise Bay

• Invercargill Visitor
Information Centre
Queens Park
108 Gala St
Tel: (03) 214 9133

Te Anau
•Fiordland Visitor Information
  Centre
  Lake Front Drive
  Te Anau
  Tel: (03) 249 8900
Wellington
•NZ Tourism Board
  89 The Terrace
  Fletcher Challenge House
  Wellington
  Tel: (04) 472 8860

Whakatane
•Whakatane
  Information Centre
  Boon St
  Whakatane
  Tel: (07) 308 6058

INTERNATIONAL
In Australia
•NZ Tourism Board
  Level 8, 35 Pitt St
  Sydney 2000

Tel: (02) 9247 5222
www.nztourism.com.au
In New Zealand
•Australian Tourism
  Commission
  Level 13, 44-48 Emily Place
  Auckland 1
  Tel: (09) 379 9594
  Fax: (09) 307 3117
  Email: myates@atc.
  gov.au
  www.aussie.net.au

CONSERVATION & RESEARCH ORGANISATIONS

This list includes organisations that are involved in cetacean research, education and conservation, such as natural history museums, along with their contact details and web sites (listed
with the www. prefix). While not exhaustive, it will provide you with a starting point.

AUSTRALIA
•Antarctic Adventure Centre
  2 Salamanca Sq
  Hobart 7000
  Tel: (03) 6220 8220
  or 1800 350 028
  www.antarctic.com.au
•Australian Antarctic Division
  Channel Hwy
  Kingston 7050
  Tel: (03) 6232 3209
  Fax: (03) 6232 3288
  www.antdiv.gov.au
•Australian Dolphin Research
  Foundation
  PO Box 572
  Magill 5072
  Tel: (08) 8390 3554
  Fax: (08) 8390 3526
  Email: bossley@olis.
  net.au

•Australian Mammal Society
  Dept of Anatomical Sciences
  University of Adelaide
  Adelaide 5005
  Tel:(08) 8303 5743
  Fax: (08) 8303 4398
•Australian Marine
  Conservation Society Inc
  Level 1, 92 Hyde Rd
  Yeronga 4104
  Tel: (07) 3848 5235
  or 1800 066 299
  Fax: (07) 3892 5814
  www.ozemail.com.au/~amcs
•Australian Museum
  Search & Discover
  6 College St
  Sydney 2000
  Tel: (02) 9320 6202
  Fax: (02) 9320 6065
  www.austmus.gov.au

•Australian Whale
  Conservation Society
  PO Box 12046
  Elizabeth St
  Brisbane 4002
  Tel: (07) 3824 8778
  or 0411 406 939
  Fax: (07) 3824 8636
•Carnarvon Whale Museum:
  see Carnarvon Tourist
  Bureau, WA
•Dept of Conservation &
  Land Management (CALM)
  50 Hayman Rd
  Como 6152
  Tel: (08) 9334 0333
  Fax: (08) 9334 0432
  www.calm.wa.gov.au
•Dept Environment, Heritage
  & Aboriginal Affairs SA
  GPO Box 1047

Adelaide 5001
Tel: (08) 8204 9000
Fax: (08) 8204 1919
• Dept Natural Resources &
the Environment
8 Nicholson St
E. Melbourne 3002
Tel: (03) 9637 8000
Fax: (03) 9637 8150
www.nre.vic.gov.au
• Dolphin Research
Project Inc
PO Box 1245
Frankston 3199
Tel: (03) 9783 7466
Fax: (03) 9783 7048
Email:dolresin@
iaccess.com.au
www.dolphinresearch.org.au
• Earthwatch Australia
126 Bank St
South Melbourne 3205
Tel: (03) 9682 6828
Fax: (03) 9686 3652
www.earthwatch.org
• Eden Killer Whale Museum
94 Imlay St
Eden 2551
Tel: (02) 6496 2094
Fax: (02) 6496 2024
• Environment Australia
Biodiversity Group
GPO Box 787
Canberra 2601
Tel: (02) 6274 1111
Fax: (02) 6274 2314
www.erin.gov.au
• Environment Protection
Agency
288 Edward St

Jetset Building
Brisbane 4000
Tel: (07) 3225 8818
Fax: (07) 3225 8723
• Greenpeace Australia
Level 4, 39 Liverpool St
Sydney 2000
Tel: (02) 9211 4066
Fax: (02) 9261 4588
www.greenpeace.org.au
• Humane Society
1/74 Old Barrenjoey Rd
Avalon 2107
Tel: (02) 9973 1728
Fax: (02) 9973 1729
www.hsi.org.au
• Museum & Art Gallery
Northern Territory
Conacher St
Fannie Bay 0820
Tel: (08) 8999 8201
Fax: (08) 8999 8289
www.nt.gov.au/dam/
magnet/index.shtml
• National Parks &
Wildlife Service NSW
43 Bridge St
Hurstville 2220
Tel: (02) 9585 6444
Fax: (02) 9585 6527
www.npws.nsw.gov.au
• Oceania Project
PO Box 646
Byron Bay 2481
Tel: (02) 6687 5677
Fax: (02) 6685 8998
www.oceania.org.au
• ORRCA (Organisation for
the Research & Rescue of
Cetaceans in Australia)

PO Box 442
Artarmon 1570
24-hour strandings hotline
Tel: (02) 9415 3333
Fax: (02) 9413 1076
www.orrca.org.au
• Parks & Wildlife Service
GPO Box 44A
Hobart 7000
Tel: (03) 6233 6556
Fax: (03) 6233 3477
www.parks.tas.gov.au
• Queensland Dept of
Environment and Heritage
PO Box 155
Brisbane Albert Street Post
Office 4002
Tel: (07) 3227 7111
• Queensland Museum
Reference Centre
cnr Melbourne &
Grey Sts
South Brisbane 4101
Tel: (07) 3840 7635
Fax: (07) 3846 1918
www.qmuseum.qld.gov.au
Friends of Queensland
Museum
Tel: (07) 3840 7632
• Scienceworks
2 Booker St
Spotswood
Melbourne 3015
Tel: (03) 9392 4800
Fax: (03) 9391 0100
www.mov.gov.au/sw
• South Australian Museum
Information Section
North Tce
Adelaide 5000

Tel: (08) 8207 7500
Fax: (08) 8207 7222
www.samuseum.sa.gov.au
• West Australian Museum
1 Francis St
Perth 6000
Tel: (08) 9427 2700
Fax: (08) 9427 2882
www.museum.wa.gov.au
Friends of WA Museum
Tel: (08) 9427 2719

NEW ZEALAND

• Dept of Conservation/
Te Papa Atawhai
cnr Karangahape Rd &
Liverpool St
Auckland
Tel: (09) 307 9279
Fax: (09) 377 2919
• Dept of Conservation/
Te Papa Atawhai
59 Boulcott St
Wellington
Tel: (04) 471 0726
Fax: (04) 471 1082
www.doc.govt.nz
• Greenpeace New Zealand
Private Bag 92507

Wellesley St
Auckland
Tel: (09) 630 6317
Fax: (09) 630 7121
www.greenpeace.org.nz
• Museum of New Zealand/
Te Papa Tongarewa
Cable St
Wellington
Tel: (04) 381 7000
Fax: (04) 381 7070
• Project Jonah New Zealand
PO Box 8376
Symonds St
Auckland
Tel: (09) 302 3106
Fax: (09) 521 5425
Email:pj@wildside.gen.nz

INTERNATIONAL

• International Whaling
Commission
The Red House
135 Station Rd
Impington Cambridge
England CB4 9NP
Tel: 44 (1223) 233 971
• Pacific Whale Foundation
Suite 25

Kealia Beach Plaza
101 North Kihei Rd
Kihei, Maui
Hawaii 96753 USA
Tel: 1 (808) 879 8811
• Pieter Folkens
A Higher Porpoise
Suite F
940 Adams St
Benicia California
94510-2950 USA
Tel: 1- 707-746 1049
Fax: 1-707-746 5599
Email: animalbytes@
earthlink.net
(Contact Pieter Folkens for
posters of his illustrations
of cetaceans featured in
this book.)
• The POD – People Oceans
Dolphins
Dr Jason Cressey
304/1928 West 2nd Ave
Vancouver BC Canada
Fax: (604) 734 1108
Email: Canadaorca@
hotmail.com
www.premier1.net/
-iamdavid/ocean.html

FURTHER READING

• Baker, A.N. *Whales and Dolphins of New Zealand and Australia*. Victoria University Press, Wellington, 1983.

• Bannister, J. *Western Australian Humpback and Right Whales. An Increasing Success Story*. WA Museum, Perth, 1994.

• Bannister, J.L., Kemper, C.M., and Warneke, R.M. *The Action Plan for Australian Cetaceans*. Australian Nature Conservation Agency, Canberra, 1996.

• Carson, R. *The Sea Around Us*. Oxford University Press, New York, 1951.

• Carwardine, M. *Whales, Dolphins and Porpoises. The Visual Guide To All The World's Cetaceans*. Harper-Collins, Sydney, 1995.

• Carwardine, M., Fordyce, R.E., Hoyt, E. and Gill, P. *Whales, Dolphins & Porpoises*. Reader's Digest, Sydney, 1998.

• Colgan, K. *"Encounters With Whales 95. Conference workshop summary report."* Australian Nature Conservation Agency, Canberra, 1995.

• Cressey, J. *"Making a Splash in the Pacific: Dolphin and Whale Myths and Legends of Oceania,"* Rapa Nui Journal, Vol. 12 (3), September 1988, pp. 75-84.

• Dakin, W.H. *Whalemen Adventurers*. Angus and Robertson, Sydney, 1973 (first published in 1931).

• Dawson, S. *The New Zealand Whale and Dolphin Digest*. Brick Row Publishing, in association with Project Jonah, Auckland, 1985.

• Evans, P.G.H. *The Natural History of Whales and Dolphins*. Christopher Helm, London, 1987.

• Gill, P. and Gibson, L. *Reader's Digest Explores Whales, Dolphins and Porpoises*. Reader's Digest, Sydney, 1997.

• Grady, D. *The Perano Whalers of Cook Strait 1911–1964*. A.H. and A.W. Reed, Wellington, 1982.

• Grady, D. *Sealers and Whalers in New Zealand Waters*. Reed Methuen, Auckland, 1986.

• Harrison, R. and Bryden, M.M. *Whales, Dolphins and Porpoises*. Golden Press, Silverwater, 1988.

• Jefferson, T.A., Leatherwood, S. and Webber, M.A. *Marine Mammals of the World*. United Nations Environment Programme, Rome, 1993.

• Judd, M., Kemper, C., Ling, J.K. and Olman, J. *A Guide to Whales and Whale Watching in South Australia*. SA Museum, Adelaide, 1994.

• Leatherwood, S. and Reeves, R.R. *The Sierra Club Handbook of Whales and Dolphins*. Sierra Club, San Francisco, 1983.

• Martin, A.R. *Whales and Dolphins*. Salamander Press, London, New York, 1990.

• Mead, T. *The Killers of Eden. The Killer Whales of Twofold Bay*. Angus & Robertson, Sydney, 1961.

• Smith, P. *Management Manual for Marine Mammals in NSW*. NSW National Parks and Wildlife Service, Sydney, 1997.

• Todd, B. *Whales & Dolphins of Kaikoura, New Zealand*. Nature Down Under/ Craig Potton Publishing, Nelson, NZ, 1991.

• Tucker, M. *Whales and Whale Watching in Australia*. Australian NPWS, Canberra, 1989.

GLOSSARY

Ambergris waxy, aromatic substance found in sperm whale stomachs, formerly commanding a very high price as a perfume fixative.

Amphipod tiny crustaceans preyed on by baleen whales.

Baleen fibrous horny plates that hang from the upper jaw of baleen whales, used for filtering prey from seawater.

Beak protruding snout.

Blaze streak of lighter pigment along the flanks.

Blow spout of water created by a whale's exhaled breath.

Blowholes nostrils of whales, found on the top of the head.

Blubber layer of fat beneath the skin, used for insulation and energy storage.

Bowriding riding in the pressure wave at the bow of a boat or a large whale.

Breach act of leaping clear, or nearly clear, of the water.

Bull adult male.

Bycatch any animals, not the target species, accidentally taken by a fishery.

Calf young cetacean that has not yet been weaned.

Callosities patches of thickened skin on the heads of right whales, usually inhabited by whale lice and barnacles. Unique patterns allow recognition of individuals.

Cape darker region of skin on the backs of many cetaceans.

Cephalopods group of molluscs containing squid, octopus and cuttlefish.

Cetacean marine mammal of the Order Cetacea, which includes all whales, dolphins and porpoises.

Chevron V-shaped marking at the back of the head seen in fin and other whales.

Coaming raised splashguard just in front of the blowhole in some cetacean species.

Continental shelf shallow coastal region, generally at less than 200 metres depth.

Cookie-cutter shark small shark that takes icecream-scoop-sized bites from cetaceans.

Copepod very small schooling crustacean consumed by right and sei whales.

Cow adult female cetacean.

Dorsal pertaining to the upper surface of the body.

Dorsal fin raised fin on the backs of many cetaceans.

Drive fishery hunts of dolphins or small whales in which they are driven ashore by boats into bays, and killed.

Dugong aquatic mammal of the order Sirenia; also called a sea cow.

Ecology study of living things in relation to their environment.

Flipper flattened forelimb, supported by five skeletal digits.

Echolocation use of echoes from a directed beam of sound to locate objects.

Falcate hooked, as in the shape of a falcon's wing (applied to dorsal fins).

Flukes boneless, horizontally flattened tailplanes used for propulsion.

Fluke-up type of dive in which the flukes are raised above the surface.

Gulp feeding method of feeding used by most rorquals, in which a whale ingests a mouthful of prey by lunging suddenly with its mouth wide open.

Herd group of mammals, often used in the context of small cetaceans (also school).

Hydrophone underwater microphone used for listening to cetacean sounds.

Juvenile after the calf stage, not yet mature.

Krill small swarming crustaceans, an important food for baleen whales.

Lobtail slapping the tail flukes loudly on the surface.

Logging lying quietly at the surface.

Mandible lower jaw.

Mass stranding stranding in which three or more cetaceans are involved.

Median ridge raised ridge on top of the head of rorquals, in front of the blowhole.

Melon bulbous fatty forehead of many toothed whales, which focuses the sound beam used in echolocation.

Mysticete baleen whale.

Oceanic of the ocean lying outside the continental shelf.

Odontocete toothed whale.

Parasite an organism that exploits another animal by living on or in it, without benefit to the host.

Peduncle tail stock; that part of the body between the dorsal fin and the flukes.

Pelagic deep-sea; pertaining to life beyond the shallow tidal zone.

Photo-identification photography of recognisable features of individual cetaceans used to identify them.

Phytoplankton plant plankton, the basis of the marine food web, on which zooplankton feed.

Pod group of whales behaving in a coordinated manner.

Population group of interbreeding individuals of a species, isolated from other such groups.

Porpoising travelling efficiently at speed by leaping clear of the water.

Rakes long parallel scratches caused by teeth scraping over skin.

Range normal distribution of a species.

Remoras small fish that attach themselves to cetaceans.

Rorquals family of baleen whales that have extendable throat grooves for feeding. They include blue, fin, sei, Bryde's, minke and humpback whales.

Rostrum upper surface of the head of a cetacean, above the mouth.

Saddle light-coloured patch just behind the dorsal fin of some toothed whales.

School another term for a herd, used for dolphins or small whales.

Skim feeding method of feeding often used by right and sei whales, in which whales swim steadily at the surface through prey patches, filtering prey as they go.

Small cetaceans term given to dolphins, porpoises and the smaller toothed whales.

Song repetitive sequences of sounds produced by whales, especially humpbacks, used for communication, probably to attract prospective mates.

Spermaceti superfine, formerly valuable oil found in the melon of a sperm whale.

Spy-hopping raising the head vertically from the water for better above-water vision.

Stock synonym for a biological population.

Stranding when a cetacean comes ashore, alive or dead.

Throat grooves or throat pleats folds of skin on the throats of baleen whales that expand when feeding to enlarge the mouth.

Tubercles raised knobs or lumps, such as those on humpback whales' heads.

Vagrant animal that strays well outside its normal range.

Ventral relating to the undersurface of the body.

Whale lice cyamids; small crustaceans adapted to living on whales. They feed on dead flaking skin.

Ziphiid beaked whale of the Family Ziphiidae.

Zooplankton small animal plankton such as krill and copepods.

INDEX

PHOTOGRAPHIC ACKNOWLEDGEMENTS

Abbreviations: AE = Aurora Expeditions; AI = Auscape International; HHNZ = Hedgehog House New Zealand; NF = Nature Focus; NHIL = New Holland Image Library.
Photograph positions: t = top; b = bottom; l = left; r = right.

All photographs by Peter Gill ©, except for the following:

Shaen Adey/NHIL: pp. 1, 89, 96, 99, 101, 102, 105, 113, 124, 127; Kelvin Aitken: p. 13; Kathie Atkinson: p. 10 tl; Esther Beaton: p. 71; Stephen R Burnell/NF: p. 2; Dennis Buurman/HHNZ: p. 130; John Carnemolla/APL: pp. xii, 90; Cul/Greenpeace/APL: p. 26; WH Dawbin Collection: pp. 21, 22, 23; Ron Dorman/APL: p. 20; Jeff Foott/AI: pp. ix, 30-31; Deb Glasgow: pp. 66, 67 t, 73 t&b; Paul Hodda: p. 81; Curt Jenner: pp. 10 tr, 12 b; Tony Karacsonyi: p. 70; Jean-Marc La Roque/AI: front cover; Yves Lanceau/AI: p. vi; Mike McKoy: pp. 11 t, 17, 27, 29, 68, 74, 75; Mike Osmond/AI: p. x-xi; David Paton: pp. viii, 4, 9, 84; Jaime Plaza Van Roon/NHIL: p. 122; Graham Robertson/AI: p. 83; Rowlands/Greenpeace /APL: p. 25; Richard Symth: p. ii; Sue Werner/AE: pp. 16, 24; Konrathe Wothe OSF/AI: p. 64-65

Images on p. 18 prepared from NOAA Pathfinder Satellite Data and supplied by CSIRO Marine Research, Hobart.

WHALE-SIGHTING SHEET

DATE _____ TIME _____

POSITION
Latitude _____ ° _____ 'S Longitude _____ ° _____ 'E

LOCATION (if position unknown)
_____

SPECIES (if known)
_____

IDENTIFYING FEATURES eg: body size, dorsal fin size and shape, head and body shape, colour or pigment pattern, marks or scars, characteristics of blow, fluke shape and marking, tooth or baleen count if stranded.
_____
_____
_____
_____
_____

NUMBER Estimated number of animals, including calves.
_____

BEHAVIOUR eg: resting, travelling, breaching, feeding, bowriding, avoiding boat etc.
_____
_____
_____

TRAVEL Direction and speed of cetaceans.
_____

WEATHER eg: cloud cover, precipitation, wind speed and direction.
_____
_____

SEA CONDITIONS eg: height and direction of swell, presence of whitecaps etc.
_____
_____

OTHER ANIMALS NEARBY, eg: fish, plankton, seabirds, sharks.
_____
_____